D0978479

WEALTH
WOMEN
& GOD

This book surfaces for us the hidden stories of suffering and deliverance that are being lived out in the Arab world and other centers of mass migration. With deft storytelling, Miriam Adeney and Sadiri Joy Tira paint moving portraits of women abroad struggling to wrest a future out of poverty and misfortune, and finding in the process the gracious hand of God at work in their lives.

Seldom do we get stories from what the Latin Americans call "the underside of history"—those submerged voices tossed to and fro by the tidal forces of globalization. The authors do a great service in making us aware of the human plight and also of the sovereign God who goes ahead and accompanies peoples on the move.

—MELBA PADILLA MAGGAY, PhD
founder of the Institute for the Study of Asian Church and Culture
Philippines

These stories will touch you deeply. Some will move you to tears. They are records of women who leave home, many not by choice, wandering into faraway lands in search of money to feed their families and to build a better future. In the midst of the difficulties they face, sometimes seemingly insurmountable, we read of the amazing grace of God reaching out to each one—giving hope, strength, and perseverance to carry on. Ultimately, these stories testify to God's unfailing and faithful love.

—WONG SIEW LI
deputy director, Iclif Leadership and Governance Centre
Malaysia

Compelling vignettes coupled with vibrant portraits of contemporary and historic life in the Arabian Gulf make this slim volume a rich resource. From stories of women marred by unscrupulous labor contractors to women who work with dignity, the multilayered lives of diaspora workers are illuminated. Probing questions conclude each chapter, creating a valuable tool for individuals and groups. Evidence of persistence, hope, and resilience across the "deep trench between the wealthy and the poor" speak to us of God's presence in all places. The text concludes with "next steps" that nudge us toward concrete, practical outreach.

—EVVY HAY CAMPBELL, PhD
chair of the board, World Hope International

A totally engaging book. We feel the textures and see the colors of life, faith, and work intersecting in Middle Eastern cultures. We are moved to think about how we ourselves can live as creative minorities in our own cities. I could not put it down. I highly recommend *Wealth, Women, and God*.

—SAMUEL E. CHIANG, PhD
president and CEO, Seed Company

When cultures and governments close the doors to missionaries, send in housemaids. And nurses, nannies, and clerks. Millions of mobile women with a mighty loyalty to faith and family. This book describes the most transglobal migration at work in the world today. It is a female migration, with gripping stories of danger, blood, bruises, hopes, and heartbreak. Yet these women are leaving indelible fingerprints of faith. I could not stop reading.

The individual stories point to the big story of God's mission pulsing in the southern hemispheres between India and the Philippines and the Arabian Gulf region, between oil-rich nations and poor lands. Until now, few Westerners have noticed. Thank you, Miriam Adeney and Sadiri Joy Tira, for opening our eyes and our hearts.

—CATHERINE B. ALLEN, PhD
advocate for women in missions and ministry

Expert guides, Miriam and Joy take us "snorkeling" deep into the often unseen world of diaspora women in the Middle East. From their introductory "dive" onward, they convey in 3-D reality diverse glimpses of living, serving, and working as foreigners surrounded by the grace and sovereignty of God. Eye-opening and inspiring.

—LEITON CHINN
senior associate, Lausanne International Student Ministry

A great guide to stewarding the impossible situations of life. "My word shall not return void" is the constant theme in *Wealth, Women, and God*. Even in places where it would seem impossible to thrive and minister, God has his children. When they allow his light to shine through them, there is hope.

—DWIGHT GIBSON
chief explorer, The Exploration Group

The women in this book challenge and encourage readers to look up and see who God is, look around and see what he is doing, and look inside to reflect and then take action on what he wants each of us to do for his kingdom.

—CHERI PIERSON, PhD
associate professor of intercultural studies
Wheaton College Graduate School

Approaching charged topics with the grace and curiosity of well-informed guests, the authors examine broad geopolitical and economic structures, then zoom in on the intimate realities of individual women's stories. Their friendly, down-to-earth tone guides us on a tour of God's work among immigrant women in the Middle East.

—HANNAH RASMUSSEN
editorial assistant, Africa Study Bible

"Come, see a man who told me everything I did. Can this be the Christ?" An unnamed woman in the first century asked that question. Miriam Adeney and Sadiri Joy Tira show, through a series of deceptively simple stories, how women in the Middle East today are meeting Christ, then introducing others to him, just like that first-century seeker did. To marginalized women Christ still offers living water, especially guest workers from the Philippines, Africa, and India. This is happening in an improbable place: the wealthy, orthodox Muslim Arabian Peninsula. Told with characteristic grace and understated insight, these accounts exude the warmth of testimonies shared around a fire on the last night of camp.

—DAVID MARSHALL, PhD
author, How Christianity Passes the Outsider Test
editor, Faith Seeking Understanding:
Essays in Memory of Paul Brand and Ralph D. Winter

WEALTH
WOMEN
& GOD

HOW TO FLOURISH
SPIRITUALLY AND ECONOMICALLY
IN TOUGH PLACES

MIRIAM ADENEY & SADIRI JOY TIRA

WILLIAM CAREY
LIBRARY

Wealth, Women, and God: How to Flourish Spiritually and Economically in Tough Places

Copyright © 2015 by Miriam Adeney and Sadiri Joy Tira

All rights reserved.

No part of this book may be reproduced, stored in a retrieval system, or transmitted in any form or by any means—electronic, mechanical, photocopy, recording, or otherwise—without prior written permission of the publisher, except in brief quotations used in connection with reviews in magazines or newspapers.

Published by William Carey Library
1605 E. Elizabeth St.
Pasadena, CA 91104 | www.missionbooks.org

Aidan Lewis, editor
Melissa Hughes, copyeditor
Josie Leung, graphic design

William Carey Library is a ministry of
Frontier Ventures | www.frontierventures.org

Printed in the United States of America
19 18 17 16 15   5 4 3 2 1 BP500

2014 Philippine edition published by
LifeChange Publishing, Inc., Manila, Philippines

Library of Congress Cataloging-in-Publication Data
Names: Adeney, Miriam, 1945-
    Title: Wealth, women, and God : how to flourish spiritually and economically in tough places / Miriam Adeney and Sadiri Joy Tira.
Description: Pasadena, CA : William Carey Library, 2015. | Includes bibliographical references. | Description based on print version record and CIP data provided by publisher; resource not viewed.
Identifiers: LCCN 2015038861 (print) | LCCN 2015037889 (ebook) | ISBN 9780878088935 (epub) | ISBN 9780878086238 (pbk. : alk. paper) | ISBN 9780878088935 (ebook : alk. paper) | ISBN 0878086234 (pbk. : alk. paper)
Subjects: LCSH: Christian women--Religious life--Middle East. | Christian women--Middle East. | Women foreign workers--Religious life--Middle East. | Women foreign workers--Middle East.
Classification: LCC BV4527 (print) | LCC BV4527 .A34 2015 (ebook) | DDC 248.8/43--dc23
LC record available at http://lccn.loc.gov/2015038861

Contents

Leaving Home

In this book we dive into another world. Yet it is also our world—the world of human beings everywhere, the world of women in particular, the world where God works dynamically. Different, yet the same. Being the same, it reassures us. Being different, it fascinates us.

This is a book of devotion and discipleship. It features the Arabian Gulf, but it is not just a package of information about people in far places. In this book we see Jesus, the King of the universe, alive in our mind-blowing, scary, awesome era overflowing with opportunities and dangers. We explore rich texts from Genesis to Revelation framing themes vital to the global upheavals of our time.

In these pages we meet women who live with integrity and freshness even when much of their life is shaky. These women are winsome. They are blessings. Sometimes they are awesome as the life of God flows through them.

Of course, these women are quirky. Every human being is an exception. No story can be put in a box. Each one is a glimpse of a particular life, and of God's grace within it.

You can read this book alone or study it in a small group. There are questions at the end of each chapter to ponder or discuss.

The stories all begin with leaving home.

A bamboo house on stilts can be spacious if it incorporates several rooms. In the breezeway underneath, people sit and chat, sort and chop garden produce, store motorcycles, or pen up domestic animals at night. But, since there is money to be made in the Arabian Gulf, people throughout Asia and Africa are leaving those homes—bamboo dwellings, urban condos, and slum shacks alike—boarding 747s, and flying to the Middle East.

Here they may bunk in a dorm with a hundred rooms. Or in a flophouse in a work camp. Or in a townhouse shared by a group of strangers. They will have shelter. But they will not own a home.

The wealthiest country in the world is located in this region, as is the world's busiest international airport. Skyscrapers and sports arenas shoot up from what were bare sand dunes fifty years ago. Not many citizens in this region are Christians. Not much religious conversion is allowed. Yet, from the humble voices of lowly laborers, the good news that God has come close to us in Jesus spreads across the sand and the sea. In this hard place, faith is revitalized, leadership skills spiral upward, and global networks shimmer.

What is it like to be a maid in the Arabian Gulf? Or to be a nurse or accountant or pastor? To flee to an embassy for sanctuary? Or to defend those who are abused? In this book you will read true stories told in women's own words. This is not ancient history. This is how women right now are coping in the face of sweeping global pressures, how they are balancing the priorities that women have always valued—family, money, friends, creativity, God.

Choices are made—some virtuous, some foolish, some mixed. Singleness, marriage, children, and childlessness each bring special challenges. There are unjust imprisonments, beatings, stabbings, and rapes. There is racial prejudice.

There are soaring cities, boggling malls, competitive salaries, and multicultural discoveries. There are spiritual births and vibrant churches. Sounds and sights and smells waft through descriptions of economics, politics, religions, and relationships.

This book is about women far from home who are workers in the Middle East. We will trace their sufferings, spiritual growth, and service. Like Hagar, some will hear God's voice for the very first time in an arid desert country. Like Hannah, some will ache for children and see God provide in surprising ways. Like Lydia, some will be skilled businesswomen. Like Priscilla, some will train godly leaders. These Gulf women's stories, like those in the Bible, will teach lessons that apply to us in many countries.

My own grandfather, Gustav Fleischmann, immigrated to the US from Prussia, later Germany (Miriam writes). Sometimes at family gatherings Grandpa would recite narrative folk poems. One was about an immigrant who had faith in God but little else, like some women in the Arabian Gulf today. This poem included verses from the hymn "A Child of the King." I remember Grandpa singing:

> A tent or a cottage—why should I care?
> They're building a mansion for me over there.
> Though exiled from home, yet still I can sing.
> My Father is rich! I'm a child of the King!

Throughout history, Christians on the move have treasured the hope that Grandpa sang about. They remember Jesus' words, "In my Father's house are many mansions, and I am going to prepare a place for you" (John 14). Another "golden oldie" with the same theme, "I've Got a Mansion," concludes:

And someday yonder we will nevermore wander
But walk on streets that are paved with gold.

This promise packs power when you own no property as far as you can see.

Yet there is more. Not only do we look forward to our own mansions. More amazing, we ourselves are parts of a temple where God is in residence, according to the Apostle Paul (Eph 2). While the building is not finished, and continues to stretch higher, all the parts fit together even now. And we are those parts, "living stones," according to the Apostle Peter (1 Pet 2).

In the pages that follow, we invite you to read stories of women who have left home to become living stones in the Arabian Gulf. Envision the temple that is rising. Share the joy over mansions that are still being designed. And consider where you fit in this global palace under construction.

Interviews were conducted in Abu Dhabi, Dubai, Qatar, Kuwait, and Oman by Sadiri Joy Tira, Lulu Tira, and Miriam Adeney as a project of the Global Diaspora Network of the Lausanne Committee for World Evangelization. Every woman interviewed was well known to a local community of Jesus' followers. We have tried to adhere closely to each woman's words and emphases. Naturally such accounts are incomplete. Nobody tells her own story the same way twice. Also, circumstances change with time, as do perspectives. We present these narratives as true slices of life, glimpses of God's grace. We do apologize for any errors. For security reasons, most of the names have been changed.

Up every morning at 4:00 a.m. Thirty minutes' walk to school, and at the end of the day thirty minutes' walk home to a poor farm overflowing with children. Rice paddies. Banana trees. Cows chomping weeds. *Carabaos* (water buffalos) wallowing in mud holes. From a tourist's perspective, the Philippine province of Pangasinan may be picturesque. But to Chelsea it was boring. Same old, same old.

Still, she kept on with those daily walks and in due time graduated from high school. Since there was no money for college, she earned a nursing aide certificate from a technical school.

"But there is no good work in the Philippines for nurses' aides, even if you work hard," Chelsea comments. "The salary is too low. There is only enough money for you yourself. You can't support your family."

What about all those younger sisters and brothers on the farm?

"Go abroad," an aunt advised her. That woman was already working in Kuwait. "You can find a job, and you'll earn plenty."

In order to help her parents and siblings, she agreed.

This book grows out of the stories of migrant working women like Chelsea. Beyond these women's individual experiences, the narratives open a window into a larger world— namely, the 200 million people who are currently moving from the country where they were born to another country: students, refugees, businessmen, immigrants, but most of all laborers who need jobs. A human tsunami is flooding across borders. These migrations are reshaping our world. They will make a difference for all our futures.

If, as it seems, God is scattering the peoples, how should we respond? What can we learn from these "global nomads"? How might this huge multinational exchange affect Christian witness? Discipleship? Church formation? Theological education? Service to the needy? Advocacy for the oppressed? What new ethical and theological challenges arise?

This book gives glimpses of God's grace at work through some of the least powerful people in the great sweep of human labor exchanges today. We could just as easily study men in middle management who are part of this global diaspora, but we have chosen to focus on working women. Similarly, we could zero in on any region in the world, but we have chosen to direct our attention to the Arabian Gulf.

All who read this will ultimately be faced with the question, what can *we* do? In the end, that is why we have bothered to invest time in researching and writing this book. Titillation is not our goal, nor even compassion that will burn out, but rather understanding that results in action.

Chelsea's story provides some hints. It is a good place to start.

For three and a half years, Chelsea worked as part of a large Filipino cleaning crew in the compound of a Saudi Arabian princess. But she chafed at the restrictions there. Only nineteen years old, Chelsea bubbled with life. Yet the maids were forbidden to hold mobile phones unless they were given permission. They had to be covered completely. They were not even supposed to talk together. Freedom always had been important to Chelsea. Now she felt stifled. "We were in bondage," she says. "We could not have fun. It was not allowed. Life was so boring."

Sometimes when her employer was not home Chelsea would go up on the rooftop and look for a Filipina on another roof. If she saw one, she would wave and yell, "*Kababayan!* (Fellow countryman!)" Anything to transcend the boundaries.

Yet when she finally returned to the Philippines, she had gained something besides money that would make a dramatic difference in her future. She had picked up the Arabic language. Desperate to communicate, she had put out the effort to learn a little every day, using gestures to ask questions, paying attention to body language, and reviewing what she learned. When she left Saudi Arabia, she could speak and she could understand.

DAYS OFF UNLIMITED

After nine months at home with her family and the cows and the *carabaos*, Chelsea applied for another job in the Gulf. This time she became a personal maid in a private home. Yet it was not long before she felt stifled once again. Her employers didn't trust her to use the phone, or to go out, or even to stay in the house alone. Chelsea complained to friends who worked as maids in other homes. One day a Filipina named Dari challenged her to open herself to the love of God.

"I also know Jesus," Chelsea protested. "Why do you think badly of me? I'm strong enough in myself."

Dari posed a challenge. "If you are in the Lord, he will touch your employer. And you will be free. Do you see me? I'm always going out to Bible studies. And I can sleep over in my friend's house."

Why? Chelsea said in her heart. *We are both women. We are both Filipinas. For me it's work, work, work in the house. I cannot see the beauty of the world. I cannot talk with my friends except when I can snatch a rare moment. Then I wake up and do it all over again. Then I go to my room alone and wonder, What is life about?*

"You may know Jesus, but does Jesus know you?" Dari continued.

Hmm. Does Jesus know me? I'm not sure. But maybe I can take a step. Chelsea challenged God: "I will accept you if you do something for me. I want freedom. My friend is free to go out to church, but my employer does not allow me to go out."

With this challenge, Chelsea says, she submitted to Christ as Lord in November 1997. She started reading the Bible. She invited Dari to pray for her. "If our God is really alive, he can answer my prayer and give me the freedom that I want. If God is alive, he will allow me to go to the church."

She asked her employer for time off so she could go to church. The time was granted. Then she asked Dari, "What do people wear in your church? Skirts or what?"

"Anything!" Dari answered.

Chelsea remembers her first church visit. "I thought it was a crazy place. People were shouting and crying." But she wanted to return, and her boss gave permission.

The second time she attended, she heard someone remark, "Wasn't that great training last week!"

What training? Chelsea wondered.

When she learned that fellowship and teaching continued on into the evening, she decided she needed time off not simply for the worship service but for the whole day. This proved too much for her employer, who became stricter. No longer could

Chelsea communicate with friends on the phone. Nor was she allowed to leave the house.

"Why, Madam? Your husband is going to mosque. Why can't I go to church?" Chelsea asked.

"You can pray in your room," the woman replied. "You stay home. Otherwise I'll send you back to your country. I don't need you. I'll deport you."

Lord, if I don't have a job anymore, how about my family? Now, Lord, this is the time for you to do something for me, Chelsea said under her breath. Then she turned to her employer and said, "OK, if you want me to go, I'll pack my things." She was calm. She had peace that God would do something. *I will trust you. I will trust you,* she repeated over and over while she cleaned and washed.

Three days passed. Then her boss called her in. Chelsea shivered. Maybe this was it. Her boss surprised her, however. "OK, I'll allow you a full day off!"

Chelsea jumped up and embraced the woman.

Yet the struggle was not over. Her boss's curfew was seven o'clock. Some people prayed in the church until midnight. Chelsea wanted to join them. *Lord, I need the day off unlimited. Not with curfews,* she breathed. Although she was nervous about requesting the end of curfews, she did. At first her employers objected because they knew some people do wrong things on their days off. So Chelsea always told them exactly what went on in the training and the Bible studies. They relented.

"Now to the max I was fellowshipping, going with brothers and sisters, praying, Bible studying. I was satisfied, with great joy," she says.

GRATEFUL FOR AN ARAB FAMILY

Meanwhile, Chelsea's freedoms continued to expand in other areas. Originally her employers wouldn't leave her alone in the house. They didn't trust her. They had heard of maids who invited men in for visits and got into trouble. But in time Chelsea earned their full trust. Now even if they travel to Europe for weeks, they leave her in charge of the home as their house-sitter. They give her the responsibility to deposit checks and cash at the bank. They send her to the ATM to withdraw money from their account. Now she is the one who is responsible for the papers for other workers, insurance, etc. Eventually Chelsea's employers even sponsored her three brothers and their wives to come work in the Middle East. "God used my boss so that I can help my family," she says.

"Who is your employer? An Arab?" people ask. They are surprised when they hear about Chelsea's happy working conditions. "Many people say Arabs are bad people. But that is not true," Chelsea says. "Even us, when we are not born again, our attitudes are not good. And the same for them. God taught me patience and love here. Sometimes they talk so fierce and they are rude and really bad. But if you are with the Lord you can cope with these things. You learn to trust God and maintain a Christ-like attitude. My testimony is what God has done in my relationship with my boss. We have become like sisters. She knows me and I know her. If you put Jesus at the center of your life, everything will be OK. I'm grateful to work for this Arab family."

As a result, Chelsea has had many opportunities to talk about her faith in that home.

"You are really different from others. There's something in you," her employer tells her.

"I believe Jesus is alive," Chelsea answers.

"Oh yes, and he will return to earth," says her employer.

"Oh really? You believe that?"

"Oh yes, but Prophet Muhammad too."

"No, Madam, we believe Jesus is the Lord above all, and we need to believe in him because he died on the cross and paid the penalty for our sins."

"No, they told me somebody else died on the cross."

Chelsea repeats that it was Jesus who died on the cross and paid the penalty for our sins, and we must trust in him to have eternal salvation.

"No," says her employer. "For us, we have to do good works, and if the balance is favorable we will be saved. "

"No," Chelsea responds. "For us, we cannot depend on our good works but on the grace of God."

"No, the thing is, you need to do good. That's it, Chelsea."

"No, Madam, I believe that only Jesus can save us, not all these good works."

CREATED NOT JUST TO RELAX

Although she is a maid, Chelsea has been able to finish a Bible college degree during her time in the Gulf. The International Institute of Church Management is a program that was set up by an Indian Christian. It offers courses in Scripture—Old Testament, New Testament, Pauline writings, etc. It also offers classes in counseling. Chelsea began with another local Bible school, but when she found that it had no accreditation she switched to the IICM.

"Madam, I want to study to go deeper in my faith in God," Chelsea explained when she requested permission to begin this course. "I want to finish a degree. It will take three years, three evenings every week." Her boss gave permission. So for three years Chelsea attended classes. This also required cultural adjustment, since all the students in the early classes were Indians.

"The Bible school made me stronger. It helped me to know a lot more about God. And the more you know God, the more you will trust him," Chelsea says. She also learned about being prompt. Students were marked down if they were late. She learned to discipline time with God. "If you want to grow in the Lord, you need discipline," she says.

The teachers were tough. They were also personal. Periodically a teacher would phone her. "What is the message of God for you right now? What is he teaching you today?" he would ask. Although this teacher has moved to a nearby country, Chelsea still consults with him by phone, and he still asks her pointed questions. And those Indian fellow students who once seemed strange have become true friends. She visits them in their homes.

Now and then Chelsea is asked to preach. Lately she has been preaching on the topic of why God created us. Not long ago she preached at a basketball camp that included a mix of believers and unbelievers. "God created us for service, not just to relax, but to serve him," she says.

She has even gone on short term mission trips to Kenya and India. "Madam, we have a mission to this place, and I need to go there," she explains to her boss. "This is the date I will leave, and this is the date I will return." And they give her their blessing. For mission work within the country, she often has the use of their car.

Chelsea does one-on-one discipleship with members of the church, members of her Bible study, and members of her family who are employed in the same household. "Before we sleep we pray and reassure each other. My two sisters-in-law are still new in the Lord," she says.

Among the house employees was a maid from Indonesia named Iman. One Good Friday, while the boss was on vacation, Chelsea asked Iman, "Would you like to come to church with me?" Iman said yes. Dressed in the *traditional Muslim* full-body covering, she accompanied Chelsea to the worship service. Afterwards, the Filipinos at church tried to talk with Iman. But she didn't speak their language.

How will I share the good news with her? Chelsea wondered. *She's illiterate. Our only common language is Arabic. Lord, help me share.* Then, speaking in Arabic, Chelsea acted out the gospel step by step.

A few nights later, Iman had a dream. Early in the morning she rushed into Chelsea's room. "Wake up. Chelsea!"

"Huh?" Raising her head from the pillow, Chelsea shook herself to clear the fuzziness from her brain.

"I dreamed about Jesus." Iman's eyes were big. "I was riding on a white horse, and he called to me."

Suddenly Chelsea was wide awake. "What did he say?"

"He's saying 'Come.' And I'm afraid."

"Don't be afraid. He loves you."

"OK." Iman opened her heart and gave her loyalty to the Lord Jesus Christ. She quit praying the memorized Arabic

Muslim prayers, and instead prayed daily with Chelsea during the twelve years that Iman continued on in that household.

Meanwhile, in spite of her cosmopolitan contacts, Chelsea has not forgotten that poor farm with the cows and the *carabaos*. Besides finding jobs for her siblings in the Middle East and discipling them, she has also witnessed to her family back in the Philippines and encouraged them. "I desire that everybody in the family will deepen their relationship with God," she says. "Praise God, in their old age my parents are active. There is a Bible study in their house. Mother has donated a chair to the church. And she cooks for church events although she is old and sometimes doesn't feel well."

Chelsea dreams that someday there may be a church on her own family's land. Their relatives will come and worship the Lord. "I desire that all of us will serve God. One day, maybe." She dreams with Joshua: "As for me and my house, we will serve the Lord" (Josh 24:15).

YOU ARE THE LIGHT

Once, when Chelsea's contract was about to expire, her friends urged her to get out of that house.

"But my employer wants me to renew my contract. And they've treated me very well," Chelsea protested.

"Yes, they like you now, but that could change," her friends warned. "Anyway, why not get a job in a business? You have enough experience and contacts and language to make the switch. A business job pays more. And you'll have more freedom. Nobody will boss you around day and night."

Chelsea's Christian friends asked a different question. "What is God telling you? When you led prayer last month, you quoted Matthew 5:18 about being a light before men . . ."

"Yes," Chelsea decided. "I don't feel I've witnessed enough to this family. I need to sign another contract with them."

Originally she was the nanny. When the children were younger, she showed them the Jesus film in Arabic. Now her "little boy" is sixteen years old, but he still talks with her. "What kind of Christian are you?" he asked recently.

"I'm a born-again Christian," she answered. "I'm not worshipping with images. I'm worshipping God directly. I received Jesus into my heart, and I know that he is alive, and that all people will worship him."

"But Prophet Muhammad also will save us. And I'm doing good," argued the teenager.

Commenting on this, Chelsea says, "I cannot convert them. I will do my job, and God will do the rest."

Since the children no longer need a nanny, Chelsea now is designated as the family's driver, but in fact she fulfills diverse responsibilities. She knows the whole extended family of her employers and prays for them. "Even the parents of my boss, when they come to visit, they want to see me. If I'm not here, they know that I'm doing my ministry." At celebrations she is seated with the family and served with them. She has worked for them now for sixteen years. At one point she retired and went home to the Philippines, but eventually the family persuaded her to come back. Although they have heard the gospel many times, she stays to shine as a light among them.

Beyond her employers' family, Chelsea says, "I desire that this country will come to know God." In this multicultural nation, 70 percent of the work force comes from outside. Chelsea is fluent in both English and Arabic, the most widely used languages. She finds opportunities to share her faith with all kinds of people.

Chelsea has never yearned for a husband and children of her own, but she would love to serve the Lord full time and go to other countries. She is waiting for the right time. "If you wait upon the Lord, you will soar like an eagle," she smiles as she moves her arms up and down like a bird flying in the air.

Esther is Chelsea's favorite Bible character. God used Esther to free her people. Even though her life was in danger, the favor of the Lord was with her. Chelsea's email address is Estheralive. Her favorite Bible text is John 8:36: "If the Son will make you free, you will be free indeed." If you are "in Jesus," she says, "every corner of your life has freedom. Even if you have an Arab employer, no one can stop the work of God in your life. If you want to serve God, he can do the things that you desire."

MADAM, I ALSO AM A HUMAN BEING

A woman takes a risk when she accepts a job as a maid in the Gulf. Some have been raped. Many have been beaten or slapped. Nearly all have been deluged under torrents of tongue-lashing. In some homes refrigerators are locked and maids don't get enough to eat. Other employers delay paying maids, sometimes for months. What can women do when these things happen? Where can they go? Even to leave the country, they need their employer's signature.

By contrast, Chelsea blossomed. It was as a maid in the Gulf that she encountered God in Jesus. It was here that she grew in her knowledge of God and of Scripture and of Christian leadership skills. Today she blesses others through a range of competencies that she learned while she was employed as a maid. In the home where she works, she has become known for her integrity, her care, and her joy. As a result, like Daniel in the Babylonian and Persian civil service, Chelsea is a highly trusted overseer in her employers' domain.

While her first years in the Arab world left her bored and frustrated, today Chelsea drives her employers' BMW even on her own ministry errands, takes charge of their ATM card, and has the freedom to make international short-term mission trips. Arabs can be good employers, Chelsea says. She also has suggestions for others who plan to work in the Gulf.

First, prepare yourself before you come. Prepare not only physically but also spiritually. Otherwise you may forget God when you have been here for a while. You may forget the goodness of God. That's the consequence if you are not prepared for what you will face. You may become a dishonor to God. Always seek first the kingdom of God. Keep that central. Then pray that God will give you an employer who will treat you well.

Second, learn about Arab culture and everyday life. Learn about their customary behaviors. For example, Arab voices are very loud. To Filipinos, this kind of talking sounds angry. But often it is just an employer directing a maid to do a task. The employer is not angry. Chelsea has learned to ask, "Madam, are you angry at me or are you just asking me to do something?"

"I'm not angry. I just want the job done," her boss will answer.

Third, learn a little Arabic. Learn the most common words. Learn basic household words. You'll be scolded less. If the boss has gone to the trouble to sponsor you and is paying you good money, and then you can't understand what she says, is it any wonder if she loses her temper?

Fourth, get some experience doing household work. Some who accept a job as a maid never have kept house back home. Other people in their extended households have taken care of those chores. So develop some basic skills before you come. And remember that we are not working just for human employers; we are working for the Lord.

Fifth, if you are lonely as a single, or if your husband has remained back in your home country, you must find a mentor in your church here who can continue to disciple you. You must be in a relationship of accountability.

Sixth, if worse comes to worst, if you are beaten or sexually abused, you must take action. Sit with your boss. Explain the situation calmly. "Madam, this is not good what you are doing to me. I also am a human being. I also get hurt. Even if I am a housemaid, I also must be treated as human."

If the employer does not change, and you are truly treated badly, you must ask your employer to go to the embassy and end the contract. Say, "I thank you so much for sponsoring me, but if you don't like my work we should end this." With a Christlike attitude bless those who persecute you and speak wrongly of you.

If the employer will not do this, some maids will run to their country's embassy and take refuge there, sometimes for months, until their passage home can be arranged.

But, Chelsea advises, don't decide at once that you have to flee. A quick decision is a bad decision. If you pray for your employers, God may change their hearts. It's possible with God. Pray first, then talk calmly. Quote or show your boss the passage in Ephesians that advises bosses to treat their servants well. Tell them peaceably and with a Christ-like spirit, "You don't have the right to hurt people who are working for you, because you also have a boss in heaven. The Quran too says we should treat people well."

Maybe the beating situation can be a step to sharing the gospel with your boss. Ask God: "Lord, is there something that you want me to do here?"

Bible Study Discussion Guide

1. What kinds of freedom does Chelsea experience today? Is she freer than when she first came to the Arabian Gulf?

2. How did Chelsea take initiative to increase her freedom? Think of worship, Christian training, mission, witness, family ministry, etc.

3. When you don't feel free, what can you do about it?

4. What kinds of freedom should you expect?

Read and discuss these texts about
FREEDOM:
John 8:36 and Galatians 5:1,13–22

CHAPTER TWO

The Wealth

Oil seeped out of the rock. Viscous, slick, and shiny, it slithered and spread. The slime trickled down into a crack, greasy, dark, and smelly.

But nobody paid much attention.

For thousands of years, men like Abraham paced past. Lifting their walking sticks rhythmically, then setting them down in the sand, they squinted through the dust to eye their caravans, evaluating the camels' health, judging the loads' arrangement, worrying about details at the destination but also gloating over profits to come. In the evenings they brewed coffee at a campfire and reclined around the blaze. Poetry came easily, both time-tested verses and new lines. In the morning, some murmured prayers, bowing heads and raising hands to heaven, before shaking the sand from their garments and resuming the journey.

Meanwhile, oil oozed at their feet, almost unnoticed.

Why do migrant workers flock to the Arabian Gulf today? Because there are jobs, and there are jobs because there is money from oil. It was not always so. In earlier times, Kuwaitis built boats and dived for pearls. A weighted diver might plunge fifty times a day to a depth of forty feet. Avoiding jellyfish, he would scoop oysters into a bag, then tug the rope to signal ascent. Wealth was amassed, but not by ordinary divers. Because of debt carried from one season to the next, divers were virtual slaves. Pearling seasons are remembered by their storms, feuds, raids, and sometimes plagues and famines.

Further down the Gulf, Dubai specialized in smuggling gold from India. Oman traded with Africa, including slave trading. Saudis raided camel caravans. Families that wanted to educate their sons sent them to India. Here in later centuries they would encounter the English language, British civilization, and new products. Alternatively, if they traveled to Beirut, they could absorb French civilization. India was easier to reach, however.

Yet even in ancient times oil was not ignored completely. As far back as 3000 BC, tar seeping near Baghdad was known as bitumen. People traded in it. Civilizations covered their roads with it. Today it is found in the mortar of walls in ancient cities from Babylon to Jericho. Bitumen also caulked boats. Noah may have waterproofed his ark with it. Moses' mother and sister may have prepared his floating baby basket not only with desperate hope but also with a sticky sheath of bitumen.

And people made war with it. When Cyrus the Persian took Babylon, he lit fires in the streets and threatened to add more oil if the people did not surrender. The Trojans attacked a ship with fire that could not be quenched, according to Homer. Right up to the present, oil still feeds war. If Saddam Hussein's invasion of Kuwait in 1991 had succeeded, reportedly he would have controlled 20 percent of the world's oil. Instead, he was forced to retreat back to Iraq. As his forces departed, they set six hundred wells on fire, leaving Kuwait burning.

Oil has also evoked spiritual awe. At sites where petroleum gasses escape from the earth, it is natural to stand in wonder. Some early Middle Eastern religions capitalized on the mystery and systematized the reverence. Fire worship became central in their rituals.

In ordinary homes, oil fueled lamps when people could afford it, especially after it was refined to something like kerosene. They called it "rock oil" to distinguish it from animal fat or vegetable oil. Oil has also been used medicinally for a boggling variety of plagues, from headaches and toothaches to upset stomachs, rheumatism, and wounds. Pliny listed these in the first century BC, and oil was still being applied to all these ills in the US as late as the 1800s.

Yet oil was not making anybody rich, beyond a few sharp traders.

How times have changed. The dry little protrusion in the Arabian Gulf known as the nation of Qatar has no natural water, yet today it is the wealthiest country in the world. The average annual income per head is $91,000. In the neighboring United Arab Emirates it is $57,000. In Kuwait it is $48,000. By contrast, in the United States it is $45,000, and in Britain $35,000, according to the 2012 edition of the Economist's Pocket World in Figures. What has given rise to this amazing wealth on the edge of the desert? The slick, shiny, smelly slime slithering out of the rock. That has created the jobs that lure workers from all over the world.

THE STORY OF DISCOVERY

In 1918, a British army mining engineer named Frank Holmes was stationed in North Africa. While buying beef for soldiers in Addis Ababa, Holmes overheard a trader mention seepages on the Arabian coast. As an engineer, Holmes knew about recent oil discoveries in Texas. After the war, he set up a company to search for oil throughout the Arabian region. To procure concessions, he visited local emirs. Soon he owned wide-ranging rights to search. Eventually Holmes would become known as Abu Naft, the Father of Oil, according to Daniel Yergin in *The Prize: The Epic Quest for Oil, Money, and Power (2008, 283).*

At first Bahrain looked promising. This is a small island nation in the Gulf connected to Saudi Arabia by a causeway. Here oil trickled out of the earth in various places. The ruling sheikh was not particularly interested in oil, but very interested in locating more water. Holmes drilled for water, and found it. In exchange, in 1925 he received a concession to drill for oil. Seven years later Standard Oil struck oil in Bahrain.

On the other side of the Gulf is Iran, visible from certain viewpoints and a good prospect for oil. With three times the population of Saudi Arabia, Iran treasures a magnificent history. Literacy in the Arab world was relatively rare until recently, but Iran's written calendar stretches back 2,500 years to the reign of Cyrus the Great. His empire was the largest the world had seen. It boasted good roads, a pony express mail system, standard weights and measures, and a coherent system of laws. Medicine and architecture flourished, as did poetry and visual art. The biblical characters Daniel, Esther, and Nehemiah lived in this empire. Centuries later, the traders of the Silk Road would pass through Iran, as would the earliest known Christian missionaries to China.

Since the days of the tsars, Russia has wanted power in Iran because Iran has western seaports, which Russia needs. To limit Russia, the Anglo-Persian Oil Company and the Turkish Petroleum Company began prospecting in Iran. What a Herculean project. "Each piece of equipment had to be shipped to Basra on the Persian Gulf, transshipped 300 miles up the Tigris to Baghdad (in Iraq), then carried by man and mule over the Mesopotamian plain and through the mountains," according to *Yergin (2008, 120)*. Once the parts had arrived, a hodgepodge crew of Poles, Canadians, and Azeris from Baku struggled to put the machinery back together and get it to function. They were hardly equipped for this skilled work. "To the Azeris, even the introduction of the lowly wheelbarrow was startling, a major innovation" (120).

Insects swarmed incessantly. The workers' dorms broiled at 120 degrees. Fighting tribes did not recognize the central authority that had granted the oil concession. Raiding Shiites threatened. Local dignitaries visited frequently, asking for gifts and bribes. "The population was abysmally lacking in technical skills, and indeed the hostility of the terrain was more than matched by the hostility of the culture toward Western ideas, technology, and presence" (120).

And oil was not found. So forty tons of equipment was "dismantled, carried back to Baghdad, shipped down the Tigris back to Basra, and then transshipped to the Iranian port of Mohammerah. Eventually it would be shipped by river, wagon, and mules (as many as nine hundred) to new sites, where there were also indications of oil" (124). As all the world knows, eventually oil appeared in Iran. Meanwhile, all throughout the region, explorers were watching and listening and learning from each other.

Just across the Gulf, the strong man who would become the ruler of Arabia was not particularly interested in oil. Nor was he eager for foreign explorers. They might disrupt traditional values. Ibn Saud came from the Nejd, the central and most highly regarded region of Arabia. During a two-year feud with another family, his parents travelled as nomads, packing little Saud in a bag suspended from the side of a camel. In his teen years they lived with the Emir of Kuwait. Here Ibn Saud learned the art of governance. When he was twenty, the family's enemies attacked Kuwait. As a diversion, Saud's father sent the young man back to Arabia to try to take the capital city, Riyadh. By combining stealth and force, Saud succeeded. He snuck into the city at night and executed the governor at dawn. He was proclaimed governor of the Nejd at age twenty-one.

While very conservative religiously, Saud practiced tolerance politically. When he absorbed the big al-Hasa oasis in Eastern Arabia, this included a large population of Shiites. They felt a tie to Iran because Shiism is the major type of Islam in that country. Although Saud's conservative branch of Islam criticizes some Shiite beliefs and practices, Saud granted them freedom to worship as long as they were orderly. By 1932 he had expanded his control enough to change the region's name from Kingdom of Hejaz and Nejd and its Dependencies to Saudi Arabia.

His main source of income was the travelers who arrived during the annual pilgrimage to Mecca. His expenses included regular subsidies for tribal leaders, new public works like a water system for the city of Jidda, a new radio network for the region, and luxury cars and other comforts for his kin. He wondered: Could oil bring in money?

However, like the sheikh of Bahrain, Saud was more concerned about water. An American engineer regaled him with stories about tapping into water in California and irrigating the desert. Saud invited him to explore Arabia. The engineer travelled 1,500 miles throughout the region. Unfortunately, he found no prospects for artesian wells.

He did find slight indications of oil, however. This was near the al-Hasa oasis. In 1933 the first two American geologists for the California-Arabian Standard Oil Company arrived. They grew beards, put on local headdresses and robes, and set off into the desert on camels, accompanied by guides and guards. Departing in September, they planned to return in June. During their travels they lived off the gazelles and birds that they shot, or sheep that they bought from passing nomads. Eventually they procured a one-engine plane. In order to take photos of the land directly beneath the plane, they cut a hole in the floor. Then they flew straight parallel courses six miles apart, looking out the windows and drawing everything they could see over a distance of three miles in each direction.

For five years there were only hints of oil. Then in March 1938, oil was struck in Saudi Arabia. (It had been discovered in Kuwait one month earlier.) A pipeline was laid, linking the field to a terminal on the coast. In 1939, Ibn Saud and his retinue piled into four hundred cars and drove across the desert to the oil field at Dhahran. Here they erected 350 tents. Saud swiveled the valve, and the first oil trickled out of Saudi Arabia. The story is told in detail in *The Prize (Yergin, 2008)*.

Then World War II erupted and the flow of oil sputtered. Although numerous wells had been discovered, many were cemented shut now. This was to keep them from falling into the hands of the Axis if that force overran the region. Oil did not flow in quantity until the 1950s and 1960s. Suddenly the vastness of the Arabian resource shocked the world.

ARABIA REBORN

Life was transformed. Soon, from sites that had been sand
and tents and fishermen's huts, legions of skyscrapers stretched
upward to pierce the sky. Many curve gently like ships' sails,
some white, some blue, and some glass. The world's tallest tower
stands in Dubai in the United Arab Emirates. At ground level,
huge airports showcase hundreds of planes owned by local
airlines like Emirates. Dubai's hub has overtaken London's
Heathrow as the world's busiest international airport. Though
it once lured passengers with a one-million-dollar raffle, the
chance to win a Porsche, or a month-long shopping spree, it no
longer needs such gimmicks. Within eight hours of two-thirds
of the world's population, it is a natural center.

Previously literacy was not widespread in this region. Now
schools have been built everywhere, both for boys and for girls.
Foreign universities have been invited to establish branches.
In Qatar alone, Georgetown, Cornell, Carnegie Mellon,
Northwestern, Texas A&M, and Virginia Commonwealth
universities offer classes that can be combined in an overarching
university, Hamad Bin Khalifa University. In the UAE,
more than forty international universities are licensed by the
Commission for Academic Accreditation. Their branch classes
employ the same syllabi and standards as classes in the home
countries. While the professors often are visiting faculty, local
faculty are being cultivated as well. Mixed-gender classes and
academic freedom are increasing. Modernization does not mean
Westernization, however. Qatar University recently announced
that it would switch the language of instruction from English
to Arabic.

When the Louvre Abu Dhabi opens in 2016, it will display loans from twelve French museums including Musée du Louvre, Musée d'Orsay, Musée du Quai Branly, and Centre Pompidou. These will supplement Middle Eastern art, both ancient and modern, as well as other global exhibitions spread throughout the museum's 450,000 square feet. In Qatar, the fortress-like Museum of Islamic Art extends into the blue Gulf waters. It aims to be the foremost institution in this field, educating as well as preserving. An official patron with a degree from Duke University, Sheikha Mayassa Al Thani of Qatar has been dubbed by *Economist* magazine "the art world's most powerful woman"—at age twenty-nine! She has deep government pockets, and is willing to reach into them to spend for art.

Unless controversies upset the plan, the World Cup Games will be hosted by Qatar in 2022. This is an amazing coup for the Arab world, and for this region in particular. Wealthy men from the Gulf have invested deeply in sports, both locally and globally. In the UK, for example, the Manchester City Football Club is owned by an Emirati. Horse racing around the world increasingly is dominated by Gulf owners.

In public shopping malls, wide marble floors stretch toward the horizon. High ceilings soar above rows of tall palm trees and fountains. Dior and Armani creations shimmer in the shops. Men in spotless white robes and headdresses and women in silky black designer robes languidly swish past. Portly, begowned middle-aged couples hold hands as they amble along. Small groups of teens pulsate and vibrate, the girls' jeans peeking out beneath their black scarves and tops.

The Ibn Battuta Mall features several large wings. Each showcases the architectural style of one of the regions through which that historic explorer travelled during a life that spanned from 1304 to 1369. My favorite is the Persian wing. Its center is a gorgeous blue tiled dome with a diversity of designs more complex than any mosque I have visited. Ironically, this dome arches over a Starbucks Coffee shop. Perhaps women who rarely visit mosques can imbibe a little of the beauty of those buildings secondhand while also imbibing their coffee.

Ironies do abound in this region of rapid wealth, and none is greater than the fact that most work is done by foreigners. Seventy to eighty percent of the jobs are performed by people from outside. Managers, nurses, hotel management, and certainly maids and nannies and construction workers tend to be migrants.

At the low end of the job scale is construction work. Here there are a lot of openings. New skyscrapers shoot up. Whole new islands have been created in the sea, one shaped like a palm tree and others arranged to replicate a world map. Oil wells need grunts. So does the development of civic infrastructure, from roads to schools. The World Cup games in Qatar will require a plethora of arenas. Most Gulf countries are building enormous airports. Who provides the labor for such projects? Not people who are already wealthy. They pay others to get the work done.

Construction work is dirty, dangerous, and low paid. In some places, men live in work camps, perhaps five hundred of them in an area the size of an average motel. In a room nine feet by twelve, there may be four steel bunk beds. Clearly there is not room for much else. In the dusty aisle between dormitories, propane burners sit under hot plates. Each man buys and cooks his own food unless friends share their resources and tasks. On the job site, a man must have a head for heights, because there may not be a safety cable on his skyscraper assignment.

Injuries happen, and there is little compensation. Yet migrants with college degrees take these jobs because the pay is better than what they could earn at home.

Since most laborers do not have health insurance, a migrant wife who is a medical doctor faces a long line of patients after church every Friday. She is not licensed here. Doctor slots are monopolized by migrants who speak Arabic, especially Egyptians. This woman's husband is a paramedic in a general hospital as well as a volunteer pastor. She left her career position at home to join him here. The patients who consult her now are migrants who have received minimal care from the official system. For example, an infection lasting a month may have been treated only with palliatives. She can do better. As a last resort, she can discern when to call 999 for true emergencies.

Jobs vary for women migrants, just as they do for men. If they are trained in nursing or hotel administration, they can find work in these fields. However, most openings are found at the low end of the spectrum—jobs for maids and nannies. The pay is comparatively low, privileges are limited, and abuse is a possibility.

Engineers, nurses, and executive secretaries receive the highest incomes, enough to rent an apartment, support a spouse, and raise a family while still sending money home to other relatives. Many do have children here, giving rise to several officially recognized Indian and Filipino K–12 schools. Yet there are no long-term residency options. When the children grow up, they cannot stay. Integration is not allowed. The migrants are expendable, readily discarded. By the local people they are viewed as tools. They are excluded from deep participation in the host society. Naturally this can erode a worker's sense of self-worth.

Still, the pay is more than they could earn in their home countries, so they come. Lourdes, for example, is a health fitness technician employed by a royal court in the Gulf to serve guests such as diplomats and foreign dignitaries. "As clichéd as it may sound, I chose to work abroad for greener pastures," Lourdes says. "I don't think I would work here if I were properly compensated back home." She finds meaning in church fellowship and in ministry to runaway maids.

THE JANITOR'S TALE

Fish, crabs, and prawns spilled out of Sumi's father's big boats and into trucks that stood ready to transport the catch. After fifteen days at sea, the fishermen had once again sighted the shores of Goa on the west coast of India, speedily crossed the waves, and let down anchors. They were home at last—until the next trip. This was the rhythm of Sumi's world when she was a little girl.

Having been colonized by Portugal, Goa enjoys special connections with that European country even today. Goa is the richest state in India per capita, with a flavor all its own. Here Sumi grew up by the sea. Her father ran a robust fishing business with his seven sons and two hundred employees. But as a daughter, Sumi was destined to marry out of her family and into another. Eventually she and her husband, Atul, would migrate to the Middle East in search of opportunity. There he would land a job in the Ministry of Customs.

Unfortunately, Atul had a problem with gambling. His schedule—four days on, two days off—left him with too much time on his hands. Soon he owed money. That is why Sumi went to work as a maid. Still, she made it home to Goa once a year. All her babies were born in Goa.

There was a period when her husband was back in Goa, too. They were living with their small children in his extended family's communal home. This household included not only her husband but also six of his brothers. All the demands and incessant work became too much for Sumi. She rented a small house of her own and moved out.

Money remained a problem. She had hardly any. Health was a problem, too. She suffered from bleeding that finally necessitated removal of her uterus. She worried for her children. "How are these children going to get an education?" God seemed far away. Although she had been raised in the Catholic Church, she cried out now, "Where are you, God?"

When she cried out to God, one by one her brother, her sister, and her parents brought what she needed, even though she did not tell them of her needs.

Sumi and Atul returned to the Arabian Gulf, but in time Atul was jobless again, and once more Sumi was forced to shoulder the responsibility to earn an income for the family.

"Do you know of any job in your organization?" she asked her acquaintances.

A thin, elderly Filipina named Lilit worked on a large church compound. "I think you can make a little money preparing the communion wine. We need somebody to do that," Lilit told Sumi.

Soon the church needed somebody to perform some janitorial tasks. Eventually the pastor's wife took Sumi under her wing and helped her craft a full-time position that expanded to include some employment for Atul and provided a room where they could live.

In this community, Sumi's and Atul's Christian faith came to life. I met them in their tiny apartment, where they were cooking lunch in four big pots on the stove. The room was aromatic with the smells of onions and spices. A good-sized wooden cross hung over the sink.

"Every day I sing early in the morning," Sumi told me, describing her Christian life now. "At four o'clock I wake up and kneel down and pray. I also post songs on the walls so I can remember them."

Their son is very musical, playing guitar and keyboard and other instruments. When he was born, Sumi dedicated him to the Lord. "Now that you have given me a son after three daughters, my son must be in your church," she vowed. Besides her children, her brothers are also coming to faith through her witness. "All, *all*, not only one or two," she smiles.

Still, she struggles to keep her temper, especially on the job. Some fellow workers are elevated unfairly, she thinks. And some parishioners have no consideration for the fact that she and Atul work sixteen-hour days and must rise early to prepare the grounds for the next day's events. These parishioners stand around and chatter for hours after evening worship services. When they notice that the janitors are waiting to clean up, they just shrug. "Don't worry, Sumi and Atul. God will give you strength," they say. Then they go on talking. Some don't really know God, she believes. Some even tell lies.

"When people do wrong things, my head goes crazy, there is a loud sound in my head. Some of those people, their brain is in their elbow," she snorts. Then she adds, "But God is not blind." She keeps her focus on the cross and on Jesus, "our only Savior and Lord." And no matter how exasperated she gets, she tries not to create a scene. "I ask God every day to lock my mouth."

Recently there was a forty-day fast in conjunction with the ministry of a pastor-teacher who visited from India. "He could tell stories from head to toe without looking at notes," Sumi marveled. She identified with his stories and was blessed.

The couple also accesses international broadcasts for Christian teaching. On their kitchen table lay a letter from the media evangelist Benny Hinn. "Oh yes, we send him donations," she said.

Sumi and Atul came to the Arabian Gulf to make money. After all these years, they still do not have much. But they have found grace, and community, and out of that richness they give, not only financially but with the service of their lives.

SUZI'S STORY

Suzi is a poised, slender accountant in a big firm that oversees restaurant budgets, but she did not come to the Gulf by choice. She was forced to come in order to avoid imprisonment on a charge of fraud.

Following an afternoon worship service, Suzi invited me to join her for supper. "You remind me of my grandmother," she said.

We ate in a restaurant where she dines frequently enough to keep a running tab, enjoying pasta with roast chicken, salad with oranges and goat cheese and chicken, and fried ice cream in pastry shells.

Suzi grew up in Baguio, the cool, pine-forested "summer capital" of the Philippines, where the tribal mountain cultures meet the wet rice–growing lowland cultures. In Suzi's family there were eight children. Ostensibly she came to the Gulf to earn money to help her brother who is in law school.

Actually the reason is uglier.

Two years ago Suzi was employed as an accountant for a large company. It was a good job with a decent salary and benefits and promotion opportunities. Her family was proud of her, and she was able to help them financially.

Overnight, everything changed. One morning her supervisor summoned her to his office. "Last night money disappeared," he said, frowning. "Do you know anything about it?"

"Money disappeared? No, sir. May I ask how much?"

"Nearly a million pesos."

"How—how could that happen?"

"That is what we are asking. You were the accountant of record, and you were present in the office when the money went missing."

Ultimately, Suzi and several others were accused of taking the funds because they were the ones on duty when the money disappeared. To avoid public shame outside the company, Suzi agreed to take a job in the Middle East and earn enough to pay back her share of the loss. She posted a large check with the company, moved to the Gulf, got a job, and each month sent back payments.

Eight months later, Suzi received another surprise in the form of an official message from the company. "It has been discovered that the security guard on duty was the one responsible for the theft. All your payments will be returned. We apologize for the disruptions."

Still, the "disruptions" have been considerable. Suzi lost a good job, lost confidence in the company, and suffered because she was not able to share the truth with friends or family or her new acquaintances in the Gulf.

What to do next? Suzi hasn't decided. These days she volunteers with the music ministry at her little church and also visits runaway maids who have taken refuge in the center sponsored by the Philippine government. This visiting ministry takes place every two weeks.

Suzi lives in a dorm with seventy-three other women. It distresses her that so many sleep around with men, even the married women. She counsels them to live differently, but they call her a spoilsport. Then she sees their marriages break up. Her closest friends are in the church.

ANGEL'S PAIN

Angel and her husband, Joe, pastored a church in South Cotabato in the Philippines. Both were seminary graduates.

As they waited in the local bus station one afternoon, Angel decided to make a quick trip to the restroom.

"Watch the stuff, OK? I'll be right back." She smiled, pointed with her chin at her travel bag lying on the bench, stood up, shook the wrinkles out of her skirt, gave Joe's shoulder a friendly stroke, and strode down the corridor to the end of the depot.

VAROOM! Suddenly the earth exploded. An ear-splitting roar thundered, and the ground rolled. Smoke boiled through the station. Choking coughs were drowned by shrieks of pain.

Where Angel had been sitting, a jagged crater yawned. At the bottom was Joe's mangled body.

As simply as that, she lost him.

In this region in the southern Philippines, conflicts often lead to violence. The bus station workers had been clamoring for a union. In retaliation, the owner had targeted the organizer of the labor protest. The owner hired someone to bring a bomb in a backpack into the station and set it on a bench, then stroll away. When it exploded, the labor organizer was supposed to get the blame.

Tragically, Joe and Angel sat on the bench right next to the backpack. Angel went to the bathroom. Joe died.

"But I saw the man who left that backpack!" Angel exclaimed. She identified the perpetrator.

Because of the corrupt crony network, he was not punished. Then Angel began to receive death threats.

It was time to get out.

Now Angel works in a bank in the Gulf. Here she is a shining light among her fellow workers.

"Will you pray for me?" they request.

One colleague who asked for prayer had a wife with cancer. The couple returned to their home country for treatment, but Angel kept in touch through regular emails, encouraging them and including prayers along with her friendly messages. The treatment was successful, and the couple returned.

"We can never thank you enough!" they tell her now.

Local Muslim colleagues also ask her to pray for them.

LENI'S SURPRISE

One hazard of working in the Gulf is unscrupulous labor recruiters. Leni encountered this. She was frustrated in her job as a maid because she never got a day off. "I work seven days a week," she said. "Why won't my employers give me a day off?"

Her employers, Fadi and Nadja, are Christians from Egypt. They try to treat their employees fairly, so they were surprised by Leni's dissatisfaction. It came to the surface when her pastor came to mediate the situation.

"We take her with us whenever we go to the park. When we go to the beach, she comes along," Fadi protested. "We try to treat her well. What is she complaining about?"

Maybe a day off is an individualistic Western concept. Still, while Leni does join the family on recreational outings, she remains on call as a servant at these activities.

"And it's in my contract!" Leni insisted. She stabbed her finger at the document. "Right here it says that I am guaranteed a day off every week."

"Not in my copy." Fadi shook his head. He drew out his copy of the contract, and they discovered that they were both correct. Her copy of the contract guarantees a day off. His does not.

How is this possible? An overzealous, unscrupulous labor contractor had forged Fadi's signature to the contract that Leni had received. Dishonest contractors constitute one of the hazards that threaten overseas workers. National governments can protest, but the international arena is vast and such operators are slippery.

WORKERS ARE A BLESSING AND SO IS WORK

Oil lights the world and creates jobs for the jobless. Yet a minister in one of the founding OPEC countries called oil "dung from the devil." This was not only because oil profits dug a deep trench between the wealthy and the poor in his land. It was also because citizens in oil-rich nations may fall into lazy habits and neglect to develop disciplines and structures that will maintain a healthy society long term.

Gulf countries' public relations videos feature horse racing, car racing, falconry, and other sports. High fashion, jewelry, and body care are lauded. Yet there are also some intelligent, committed citizens who recognize that wealth may be a *disincentive* to developing competencies and skills. Envisioning life after the oil is gone, they want to move their countries from a hydrocarbon-based economy to one that is knowledge based. Such visionaries in the fields of education, business, and government are working to build sustainable structures for their people. Women in particular are taking advantage of opportunities for university education.

At present most work still is done by foreigners. In a grocery store beneath skyscrapers, I observed one thin, weary, middle-aged Asian woman. Undistracted by the robes swirling behind her, she evaluated boxes of crackers and selected the cheapest brand. Clearly, her money was going back home.

Others are not so frugal. Dubai's Dragon Mart is advertised as the biggest Chinese mall outside China. There are no Dior or Prada shops here. This is where the overseas workers shop. Instead of high fashion, there are cut-price cameras, knockoff appliances, mobile phones shaped like handguns, audio Qurans that can speak the sacred text in a dozen languages, and romance-enhancing creams. And the buyer can haggle to lower the price, just like at home.

Besides money, workers may experience a number of other benefits. For example, professional advancement. New friends. Multicultural enrichment. A moral atmosphere insofar as immodesty, pornography, and nudity are not in public view as they might be in Europe, just across the Mediterranean. At least a person can find a place to start over here if they need to, like Suzi and Angel did. Travel poses risks, but it also opens the door to adventures.

Work itself is a privilege. We are called not to be idle but to use our gifts for the benefit of others, and with our earnings to bless our families and communities. And work in the Arabian Gulf is an opportunity to be on the cutting edge of the kingdom of God.

While oil lights the world, lasting light streams from the glory of God. Using an oil metaphor, Gerard Manley Hopkins highlighted this in his poem "*God's Grandeur*":

> The world is charged with the grandeur of God.
> It will flame out, like shining from shook foil;
> It gathers to a greatness, like the ooze of oil
> Crushed. Why do men then now not reckon his rod?
> Generations have trod, have trod, have trod;
> And all is seared with trade; bleared, smeared with toil;
> And wears man's smudge and shares man's smell: the soil
> Is bare now, nor can foot feel, being shod.
> And for all this, nature is never spent;
> There lives the dearest freshness deep down things;
> And though the last lights off the black West went
> Oh, morning at the brown brink eastward, springs
> Because the Holy Ghost over the bent
> World broods with warm breast and with ah! bright wings.

Bible Study Discussion Guide

1. What interests you in this story about oil and wealth?
    Where do you think God is in this story? Where might God
    be present in the movements of wealth and people today?

2. What do you learn from Sumi, Suzi, and Angel in their
    responses to difficult life situations? Discuss each one.
    How could you apply these lessons in your own life?

3. How can you pray better for migrant working women after
    reading these specific details?

Read and discuss this text about
WEALTH, PEOPLES, AND GOD'S FUTURE SOCIETY:
Isaiah 60

The Friends

For eight years, Ginger was a mistress.

A congressman walked into a bar where Ginger was working. This was in her home city in the Philippines. At that time she was holding down two jobs as well as going to school. In the mornings she dished out pastries in a doughnut shop. In the afternoons she shouldered book bags to university classes. In the evenings she served as a waitress in the bar.

One thing led to another, and she became the congressman's mistress.

Unlike Chelsea, Ginger had grown up in a very comfortable setting. Her father was a businessman in the shipping industry. Her mother was a teacher. From kindergarten through university, Ginger had studied in Catholic schools in the historic city of Cebu. Eventually she would graduate with a degree in hotel and restaurant management.

So why was she working two jobs while she was in college? She and her mother had fought (over a previous boyfriend). Ginger had moved out of the family home, determined to pay her own way, yet vowing that she would not neglect her schooling, that she would complete her university degree.

Along the way she met the congressman. He set her up in a "love nest." She was not idle there, however. After she graduated, Ginger worked for a hotel, then travelled as a flight attendant with Philippine Airlines. Then she had a baby.

The congressman paid the expenses. Their situation was not unusual. Powerful older men often hooked up with modern, educated, and cosmopolitan young women.

After her baby was born, Ginger installed a live-in nanny and continued her professional career. Besides her regular job, she owned a boutique. From time to time she also modeled clothes on ramps for fashion shows, as well as for print advertising. In time, a second baby was added to the mix. Ginger was very busy, and loved it.

Eight years flew by.

Then everything blew up in her face. The congressman's wife discovered the truth. She thundered an ultimatum: he must cut off relations with his hidden family. Her kin were powerful. He had too much to lose. So he walked away, abandoning Ginger and his children. The breakup was ugly.

"I came overseas to mend a broken heart," Ginger confesses.

Her sister had been working in Dubai. "Come out here," she invited. "It's an open place. You won't have a problem adjusting. It's a party city, just the kind of place you enjoy."

"OK, I'll spend a year in Dubai and then I'll come back home," Ginger decided.

THE THREE AMIGOS

Ginger accepted a job as a pioneer sales supervisor in a good-sized company. At that time, twelve years ago, Dubai was mostly sand, with just a few buildings. The dorms for foreign contract workers seemed to be in the middle of the desert. That was depressing. But Ginger made friends quickly. In fact, many of the Filipinos working there were from Cebu. A batch of her acquaintances had arrived just one week earlier. When they heard that Ginger was coming, they prepared a warm welcome for her. She soon felt at home. And every weekend she went out to party.

After finishing her first contract, Ginger moved on to a job as sales supervisor for a clothing shop. However, the clothes were not suitable for the country. The store closed. Ginger had no job. What to do? Without a job, she could not stay in Dubai. Yet she had two kids to feed back home. They lived with her parents. The congressman's money was gone. Ginger felt desperate.

To her surprise, she bumped into an old friend named Peter. He had been working in Riyadh, the capital of Saudi Arabia. Now he had moved to Dubai.

"Why not stay in my apartment to save money?" he said to Ginger. Peter also took in a mutual friend named Alan. Ginger had known them both during their university days. At fashion shows, Alan often had been her makeup artist and Peter had been the shows' designer. Now, although her current boyfriend was a Jordanian Arab, Ginger gratefully accepted Peter's hospitable invitation.

Unknown to her, Peter had committed his life to Jesus while he was working in Riyadh. Peter's friendship would lead Ginger to other Christians, and these friends would lead her to a personal and lasting encounter with the Lord Jesus Christ. This is the story of many migrant workers. The good news spreads through grassroots connections. Often there is no big organization. No plan. No long-term goals. People talk to each other. They express warmth and care. They share their hopes and their own circles of friendship.

Ginger's journey began with music. Every morning at 4:00 a.m. Peter played a Christian song. "I and Alan were not familiar with this," Ginger comments. "Also he read his Bible. We wondered what he was doing. It was so early to listen to music."

A few days later, Peter started to play Christian songs in the evening before they went to sleep.

Then one night Ginger and Alan were wondering what to do to occupy their free time. "We can't go out. We don't have any money."

Peter said, "Why don't we study the Bible?"

"OK. What's there to study?" she wondered.

"I'll give you a verse. You tell me what you think. We'll talk about it later," Peter said. "Here's the verse: 'Consider it pure joy, my brothers, whenever you face trials of many kinds, because you know that the testing of your faith develops perseverance. Perseverance must finish its work so that you may be mature and complete, not lacking anything. If any of you lacks wisdom, he should ask God, who gives generously to all without finding fault, and it will be given to him. But when he asks, he must believe and not doubt, because he who doubts is like a wave of the sea, blown and tossed by the wind' (Jas 1:2–6)."

But Peter didn't discuss the verse that night, and in fact days passed without any discussion. Ginger and Alan were so intrigued that they started to read the Bible whenever they had free time. One evening Ginger said, "What do you think this verse means? Let's cook dinner for Peter, since he's working late. Then we can talk."

"I know you're in trials," Peter said over dinner. "You used to have a good life. Now you have to ask me for a *dirham* to buy water. You have to ride public busses. You never had to do that before. This verse is for you." But Ginger thought, *Maybe that's just your way of interpreting.*

Then he started posting Bible verse references on the refrigerator, and Ginger and Alan would look them up in the Bible. Every night Peter would ask, "Any questions?"

Meanwhile, Ginger applied for a job with Emirates Air. She wanted to fly again. She passed quickly through the first application stages and considered this a miracle from God. But in the end she was "rejected for undisclosed reasons."

"Why, God?" she cried. At this point, there was just one week left on her visa.

"Maybe God has something better for you," Peter counseled. Alan advised, "Ginger, don't stay in sales. Go into administration. It's more stable."

"I can't type fast enough," she objected.

"Why don't you try? And pray about it," Peter said.

The next day a business called to schedule an interview for an administrative job. Her eyes were so swollen and red from crying that she felt she couldn't go out, and she turned down the interview. They said they would call again.

The day after that, the COO called her at 6:00 a.m. "This is Samir and I believe that you and I are scheduled for an interview at 8:30 in the office."

After she hung up the phone, she turned to Peter. "Pray!" she begged. "If they test me on my speed typing, I will fail."

"Yes, I'll pray, and the Holy Spirit will be with you and guide you," he said. *What is this Holy Spirit business?* she wondered.

She was hired. Then she revealed her situation. "I put my cards on the table. 'My visa is going to expire,' I said. 'If you want to hire me, you need to work on my visa right away.'"

"No problem. We can work it out," they answered. She began the job three days later. Alan also had an interview that week. They prayed. He, too, was hired. Peter rejoiced. "These jobs were given to you both. There's a purpose why you're there," he said. Up to now, they had been borrowing money and working little part-time jobs. Now at last they had enough money to throw a party!

TAKE THIS MAN FROM ME

Meanwhile, Peter invited them to a Filipino church in Dubai. "OK. We're not doing anything on Fridays anyway," they shrugged. "We'll come."

The church had an English service first, then a Filipino-language service. People were warm and welcoming even though they knew Ginger and Alan were not committed Christians. After the worship service, the two stayed for the discipleship class. This provoked more questions for Peter. Soon the three were running a Bible study in their apartment on Thursday nights—their weekend—instead of going out. Eventually they invited other friends to join them.

They visited several Filipino churches and even an African church where they really enjoyed the dancing and the music. Peter decided he wanted to become a member of his church. He wanted Ginger and Alan to accompany him to the services and maybe join the music ministry. They said, "OK. We like music." Although she was not a great singer, Ginger set aside time every Friday for the rehearsals.

They quit wanting to go out and party. They wanted to ask more questions about God even though it was summertime and so hot that their shirts were sticking to their bodies. One day Peter said to Ginger, "What do you think? Would you like to welcome the Lord into your life?"

Yes, she did want this. "Because of the discipleship classes after the services, I understood how I had hurt Jesus with my life before," Ginger remembers. "I shared this with Peter and he prayed over me." Then she realized that "although I had had a negative attitude toward born-again Christians, now I was one." She wondered why it had taken her so long to come to this point. "Even though I had had so many achievements in my life before, I still had felt all that emptiness. Why had I wasted all that time when this was where I felt fulfilled?"

Ginger still had an Arab boyfriend, Salim. It was at this juncture that he managed to lease a house. People here live either in "flats," which are apartments or condos, or in "villas," which are detached or semi-detached houses.

"OK, I have a villa now. We can move in together," Salim told Ginger.

So she moved out of Peter's flat and in with her boyfriend. "Peter told me that living with this man was not good," she says. "But I liked the feeling of being with somebody, and I'd been with him for some time."

She stayed active in the Friday music ministry and discipleship classes, and in the Thursday Bible classes.

Why don't I invite my boyfriend to the Bible study? she said to herself. So she did. "Come and learn who your God is." He was scared, but she encouraged him. "Don't worry. It will only be me and my friends. And you don't have to participate. You can just listen."

After a month, Salim was the one taking the initiative to get them to the Thursday Bible studies. He also quit going to bars on weekends.

Then someone told her, "You should be baptized."

How can I? I am not willing to give this man up, she said to herself.

After the seminar on baptism she cried because she wanted it so badly. She spoke to her pastor. "I have this boyfriend. But I want to be baptized. Is this a problem?"

"Yes. You cannot be baptized," he told her, and explained why.

I think you're right, she said in her heart.

Then her pastor gave her an option. "Challenge God. Tell God, 'Take this man from me.'"

Several times in the past she had tried to split from Salim, but she always ended up back in his arms. She didn't have the strength to leave.

"Be ready," her pastor continued. "You are called. You have to trust that God will act."

Meanwhile the Thursday Bible study group had grown from three to eight people, and all were baptized except for Ginger. At the baptism, everybody was singing and clapping, but Ginger was crying. Instead of staying to celebrate, she left the church and drove as fast as she could, shouting at God, "Why did you let me know you if I can't be baptized?"

Over the next months, people in the church prayed quietly for her. In less than a year those prayers were answered and her pastor's challenge was fulfilled. It really hurt. Ginger's boyfriend was called home to Jordan by his family because his dad was sick. Although Salim was not aware of it, he was being set up for marriage. Shortly after he left, he phoned. "I'm getting engaged tonight," he told Ginger.

"No!" she cried. "Surely there are still ways to change this. Surely it's not true." Then she remembered that she had challenged God. Because she had been attending training lectures, she asked for strength and guidance about what to do next. On Easter Sunday one year later she was baptized. That was nine years ago.

I WANTED SOMEBODY

At work, Ginger applied to be an administrative assistant, but instead was trained as a personal assistant by a very fierce Lebanese-Algerian. "I teach you this morning, you learn by noon, and by afternoon you're perfect," her mentor drummed into her. This woman turned out to be a Christian, and six months later Ginger took her place, well trained. Six months after that she received a raise and was able to buy a car. Slowly she got back on her feet. She remembered Peter's saying, "There's a purpose for your getting this job."

On Thursday evenings she had a Bible study. Peter helped her. She had moved into a building run by a Filipina. Rooms were subdivided, and she had gotten one of the small places. She invited Filipinos to her Bible study, and in time some became true Christians. Eventually she got a bigger flat and kept the living room, the *sala*, for meetings, rather than subdividing and renting rooms.

After she was baptized, people asked her, "Why don't you marry?" But even from a young age, Ginger never had been very interested in getting married.

An older Christian woman called Auntie Faith was a good friend, and she was not convinced that Ginger was uninterested in marriage. "You have to marry. You are so attractive. I'll pray for you that you'll desire to marry," Faith said.

"OK. Pray whatever you want," Ginger said with a shrug.

In time, her attitude began to mellow. "After a year, I felt so alone. I wanted someone to be with me permanently," Ginger says. "Church ministries filled a lot. And studying the Bible and asking questions. But there were moments when I wanted somebody to be with me. Auntie Faith had said, 'You have to pray.' So I said to myself, *Why not?*"

"Of course you want to marry a Christian," Auntie Faith had added. Ginger started to pray for a Christian. "I forgot to add any other criterion like he should have a job, should be older than me, and so on," she chuckles.

Two years later, when she was visiting her family in the Philippines, her sister remarked, "I just remembered something. You're Christian."

"Yes, evangelical Christian," Ginger answered.

"I don't really understand that. But what I wanted to say is—remember Pierre? He is the same kind of Christian. He plays drums for the church. You should talk with him."

"Never in my mind did I dream that I would end up with Pierre," Ginger says now. "I knew his family, and I had known him as a child. But he was ten years younger than me. Still, we enjoyed talking and being together." She returned to Dubai with sparkling eyes. "But I had sinned again," she confesses.

"I totally forgot what I had been taught, and had sex with Pierre. Then I was very sorry."

One month later, she discovered that she was pregnant.

OK, I'm pregnant. I'm in big trouble, she said to herself. At this time she was deeply active in church. She realized she had made a terrible mistake that would have bad impact. When she was two months along, she broke the news to her closest friends. She knew that eventually she would have disciplinary action from the church.

She called Pierre and told him the shocking news. But she added, "I'm not telling you this to push you to marry me, because our ages are too far apart. I won't have an abortion. I'll have the baby and I'll manage."

After that she stopped communicating with him. But he kept emailing and calling, even though it was very expensive. "You might think I'm young," he said. "Making you pregnant does not force me to marry you. But I want to marry you."

She felt relief. Now she had to tell her parents, who were taking care of her two kids, ages thirteen and eleven. How could she break the news? When she did, they "freaked out." All she could do was listen to them. Yes, she had made a mistake. But she didn't want to make more. She had "wanted to find a Christian guy. It seemed that Pierre was the one."

They had a civil wedding in the Philippines. It was hard for her family to accept. Did she force him to marry her? Some people thought so, although that was not the case. His parents, at least, always were easy to talk to.

Ginger had told the church elders in Dubai that she was getting married back home. But she felt awkward when she returned. People wondered, *Why doesn't she sing anymore?*

Why doesn't she stay after the service? Then she told the elders the truth. "Pierre and I have dealt with it personally before God, but I feel you ought to know. I want to inform you before somebody asks."

Auntie Faith sponsored a Christian wedding ceremony for them on Palm Island. They were married in a member's residence by the beach with the elders' blessing.

"But I never saw what a blessing it was to be with Pierre until we had housing trials," she says. "I thought I was strong, but he is the one who calms me when I shake, even though I am older and have been a Christian longer. He has wisdom. He has changed me."

A TRIAL IS AN OPPORTUNITY

In comparison with Chelsea, Ginger had more advantages. Chelsea was raised on a poor farm, Ginger in a sophisticated city. Chelsea is a maid and Ginger is an event planner. But Ginger stewarded her opportunities poorly. Although she achieved a certain level of professional success, she drank, flirted, fell into affairs, ran up debts, and conceived three children outside of marriage.

Then Ginger, like Chelsea, was introduced to Jesus Christ. How did this happen? Through friendships. This is the major way that migrants come to faith. The good news spreads whether anyone plans it or not. Ginger's frank and honest story shows some of the temptations and tough struggles that women overseas face. It also shows Ginger's unique pilgrimage. Every person is different, but the good news is for everyone, and often it arrives through friends.

Now Ginger and Pierre's Bible study is in a new location, with rotating leadership. Pierre has become a drummer in the church worship ministry team. Their son is two years old. Christian music vibrates throughout their flat, and Bible stories are a staple for the little one, whether read by the parents or by the nanny.

Back home, Ginger's teenage children have become vital Christians. They have welcomed Pierre and their new little brother. She prays with them over the phone and shares Bible verses. Her goal is constant and open communication, and she relates to them especially through music.

At work Ginger wears a cross to her job, though nearly all the employees in her company are Muslim. Colleagues have come to her to ask for prayer when they have had problems. But they know better than to call her with company business on Sundays because, as she tells them, "Sundays are given to the church."

What are her long-term goals? In her earlier life, Ginger mismanaged money, wasting it on parties and piling up bills on credit cards. Now she wants to live within her means, while also investing for the future. She doesn't want to run away from debts "like a lot of people did during the recession." In five years, she hopes they can return to the Philippines with enough money to start a business. She is buying a home there now. When her business gets established, Pierre will be able to launch out as a photographer, which is his dream.

She wants to be a testimony to other people. She says she doesn't have the gift of evangelism but she is an open book. She wants to share what God has done in her life, for his glory.

When people compliment her, instead of saying "Thank you," she says "It's by God's grace."

Ginger treasures the wisdom of Proverbs 3:5,6: "Trust in the Lord with all your heart, and do not lean on your own understanding. In all your ways acknowledge him, and he will direct your paths."

Her favorite Bible passage is the first verse that she heard, the text that Peter shared on the subject of trials. "In good times we tend to forget God," Ginger says. "So I take trials as opportunities to be closer to God, to be more intimate with him, to learn what he wants me to learn." James 1:2–5 remains special to Ginger:

> Consider it pure joy, my brothers, whenever you face trials of many kinds, because you know that the testing of your faith develops perseverance. Perseverance must finish its work so that you may be mature and complete, not lacking anything. If any of you lacks wisdom, he should ask God, who gives generously to all without finding fault, and it will be given to him.

Bible Study Discussion Guide

1. Ginger's story reminds us that every person's journey is bumpy. How do we see the grace of God in this story? Think of the points in your own life where God's grace has met you. Thank God specifically, point by point.

2. Following the model of Ginger and her friends, what steps could you take to share Christ with your friends?

3. How did Peter use music in the home and the church to witness? How did he use Bible verses and Bible study? Are there ways that you could do this?

4. How did the church hold Ginger to standards of righteousness, yet warmly affirm her? Could your church do this better?

Read and discuss these texts about
SPIRITUAL BIRTH:
2 Corinthians 4:5–7 and 5:17–21

From the moment that I stepped out of the Philippines, I resolved to tell people who I am. 'I am a born-again believer. Can you help me find a church?'"

When Charis arrived in the Arabian Peninsula, she was a young Christian with little knowledge of the Bible and no ministry skills or experience. Yet eventually she would co-lead a network of two thousand Christians of diverse nationalities and would mentor dozens of individuals in depth. How did this happen? She learned on location. Although Charis did not arrive with much training in Christian leadership, she had focus. She had passion. She had priorities. She accessed the training opportunities that she found. She practiced teamwork. She accepted responsibilities. She steered clear of tangents. She honed her skills, learned from mistakes, and built competencies.

Born the youngest of twelve siblings, Charis was the first to "know the Lord." Although she was in the third year of college at that time, her oldest sister dominated her life to the extent that Charis didn't feel free to attend the church of her choice. It was after she graduated and took a nursing position in the Arabian Gulf that doors of opportunity opened.

She had prayed, "Lord, bring me to a place where I am free to go to church and to know you more." Since Friday is the day of worship in many Arab countries, Charis deliberately selected a job in a section of the hospital where she would be free every

Friday. This was an unusual choice, because there were no other Filipinos in that section. All the other nurses were Arabs. Charis made it work, and she is still in that ward today, almost two decades later.

As soon as she was settled in her residence, Charis haunted the halls, looking for mature Christians. This dorm housed hundreds of workers. Charis discovered Mayette, who had been a believer for several years. The two went from room to room, inviting women to a Bible study. At that time, Charis knew only two verses, John 3:16 and Ephesians 3:20. But she was determined to grow.

In the Filipino church in that city, Charis studied the Bible even more. There was a Navigators discipleship program, and Charis loved that. Little by little, the church assigned her responsibilities. Eventually she was asked to teach a class. That pushed her to study. It was here in the church that she met Ellis, a godly man who fell in love with her, and she with him. They got married.

I FOCUS ON THE BEST

And they stayed. For the past sixteen years, Charis and Ellis have been living in the same country where they were married, witnessing to the Lord Jesus Christ and nurturing those who want to follow him. Ellis works as an office manager and Charis as a nurse. Their three children are in middle school and high school. While Charis and I talked at their kitchen table, one son strummed his guitar. A waterfall of notes cascaded from his intricate fingerwork to ripple beneath our conversation. Later, when their mother invited them to sing, the three teens harmonized their voices with the resonant blending that is possible for members of the same family. Yet these young people have no future here. They are being raised in a country where they will not be allowed to stay. For college, they must go back to the Philippines or some other nation.

Meanwhile, the couple has been reaching out to Filipinos in that land. In the city they have gone from hostel to hostel to lead Bible studies. Beyond the city, they have visited labor camps and other establishments from the border of Iraq to the Saudi border, especially focusing on the medical centers that serve expatriates in those places. Charis creates Bible studies for women nurses and technologists, and Ellis for men.

When people believe, they are gathered into groups. Charis and Ellis help them not only to pray and understand the Bible and support each other with love and care, but also to focus beyond themselves, to see the needy men and women around them, and to reach out further. The groups also develop systems that will sustain their ministries and grow them.

Steady increase is the result. A few years ago there were eight Filipino Bible studies. "Why not set a goal for more?" they said to each other. "How about aiming for twenty groups by the end of the year? That should stretch us." Amazingly, the number of groups grew to twenty in just two months. They revised their goal upward to fifty groups. And that goal was surpassed.

Training leaders is their special passion. "We value the discipleship model," Charis says. She trains women, particularly the wives of key men who are also being trained. At present she is mentoring about fifteen women, one by one. Even while Charis and I were talking, one of these women telephoned to ask for counsel, and Charis took time out to focus on this woman immediately.

In turn, the women that Charis is discipling are themselves discipling other women. "What I am doing with you, you also can do with others," she tells them. "My goal is to make you successful. Sooner or later you will do this kind of mentoring too."

Reflecting on this priority, Charis says, "I impact women here to be disciples so that if we are ever kicked out, the work will continue. Other Christian women may visit runaway maids who are taking refuge in the embassy, but I focus my attention on what I am called to do. I love cooking and even cleaning, but my mentor told me, 'Charis, others can do that.' So I focus on discipleship. Others can do the good. I focus on the best, the work that God has called me to."

NOT ONLY FILIPINOS

Several years ago God exploded their vision with a new idea: "God put us here in the Arab world not only for Filipinos but for all nationalities." Once they began to talk about it, the idea seemed obvious. They were surrounded by a kaleidoscope of diverse people, many uprooted and open to new friends and new ideas. As noted in chapter 2, 70 to 80 percent of the labor in some of these countries is done by foreigners. Construction projects call for laborers, engineers, electricians, plumbers. Oil companies need managers, accountants, and office and field personnel. Hotels need trained staff. Homes need maids, chauffeurs, and gardeners. In a region where whole new islands are being formed in the sea by human ingenuity, and where complex and enormous arenas for the World Cup are being erected and wired from scratch, a lot of laborers are required. The Arab host populations are needy human beings, too, though their needs may not be so easy to see at first glance.

"When we embraced this multicultural ministry, God opened doors for us," Charis says. First they discovered the Sierra Leoneans. Many men from this West African nation were working in construction projects. Their land had been wasted by a war of shocking brutality. Although the country was now at peace, the scars of poverty remained. The laborers' salaries in the Middle East were low, but for these Africans they were a blessing.

From his own pocket, Ellis hired a bus to collect the men from their construction camp and bring them to a worship service. They were supposed to return to the camp for their meal at 12:00 noon. Soon it became clear that this schedule was too tight. On some days it was impossible. Then the ministry was faced with a dilemma. Must these men miss their meal in order to attend church? Was that good news? They were hardworking. They were minimally nourished. They deserved to eat.

"We had to feed them, and we didn't have a budget," Charis says. "This was another 'walk of faith' for us. None of us was full time. The fellowship group was just starting. But almost inevitably, when a meal was missed, God would send somebody to feed the men. A brother would happen by and say, 'Can I provide a meal for you all?' With the provision that God gave every step of the way, we saw that we were heading on the right track."

Eventually there were two hundred African believers. As they came to vital faith, they were taught. Ellis baptized thirty-five from Muslim background. Following his calling to train, he discipled the leaders. One eventually took over as the pastor of the Sierra Leonean fellowship. Later this pastor returned home and started a church in Africa. Today there are people from several African nations who are members of this church in the Middle East.

Next, Charis and Ellis discovered Koreans. Some were living right next door. Although they didn't share any common language very well, a simple friendship grew. Eventually they learned that a few Korean Christians in the city were searching for a place where they could worship. They were able to help the Koreans find a suitable building and to partner with them in ongoing outreach. This little fellowship has grown into a sizable church. In time, Ellis and Charis' ministry would foster Vietnamese, Nepali, and Bangladeshi congregations. Altogether, the network of diaspora people they are shepherding totals about two thousand.

Culturally, there have been challenges. Odors, for example. One group of laborers stank. Charis couldn't stand it. "Sweetheart, I love the Lord, and I love these people, but their smell I really cannot take," she confided.

Ellis bought bars of soap and handed them out.

Then odors wafted up from another level. In many Arab homes, people remove shoes when they enter. These laborers— about a hundred men—also removed their socks, and those socks had been worn for a week. This was a cultural challenge, because Filipinos tend to be very clean about their persons, even those who live in slums.

"Sweetheart, we have to do something," Charis whispered. "Let them remove their shoes, but not their socks."

And so it was. Ministry is physical as well as spiritual and may crash because of small details. Yet it can be rescued with a pinch of common sense.

When Ellis and Charis began their larger multicultural ministry, it became clear that they had a lot to learn. They read books. Then they approached the pastor of a church attended by Westerners and begged him to mentor them. He said no. His schedule was full. But they persisted. He relented, and today they are bosom friends. It was from this pastor and his wife that Charis and Ellis learned a great deal about mentoring. "They have been like parents to us," Charis says.

The Filipino International Network also helped them. Among the millions of Filipinos who live and work outside the Philippines, FIN nurtures fellowship groups. Drawing on Campus Crusade training, FIN has created a brief five-level course for Christian leaders that emphasizes vital relationship with God through Christ, walking in the Spirit, reaching out to non-Christians, and consolidating and building incrementally so that advances are conserved. Through consultants' visits and conferences, leaders like Ellis and Charis receive ongoing prayer support, counseling, and strategy and ministry guidance from FIN. The FIN network was created by Sadiri Joy Tira and his wife, Lulu.

Most of all, Ellis and Charis learn from each other. She holds a job, mothers three children, and carries a full load of disciples. Still, she makes time to join her husband in ministry together. "There's a counseling appointment," he will telephone, or "There's a wedding." She reschedules her time so that she can join him. Ellis greatly values her input. Even more than working together, they talk together. Providentially, Charis can delegate routine housework to a Filipina maid who is also a sister in Christ, a disciple in the making.

THE SOCCER MOM

Juliet is another woman who became a mentor in the Arabian Gulf.

Her growth began with a crisis. "My son was very sick. He kept moving without stopping. I didn't know what to do. Even the doctor was stymied. I had to find a place to free my mind, so I slipped into a church compound. There was a bench outside, and I sat down on it," Juliet remembers.

Even though this was not her own church, the surroundings were quiet and peaceful and wholesome, and Juliet relaxed. *I'm so tired of going to the doctor, Lord,* she whispered.

Eventually her husband Martin arrived, and sat down beside her. Although he was sweaty from his soccer game, his presence comforted her.

BLAAAAT!

Juliet jumped. Eyes round with surprise, she stared at Martin. His shoulders tensed and his eyes darted to and fro, scanning the surroundings. What was that noise?

"It came from inside," he decided, nodding at the church building.

That was intriguing. What was happening in there?

"Let's go see!" she suggested.

They entered quietly at the back of the hall. An English-language worship service was in progress. Up to this point, they hadn't even known that an English congregation met in that place. In time they would discover that the blaring noise was a ram's horn, or *shofar.* The pastor blew it to begin a worship service.

Here in this church, Juliet's spiritual life would deepen. While her son's sickness was temporary, the impact of the church was permanent. Christian faith was not new to Juliet. Raised in the Catholic Church in Goa on the west coast of India, Juliet had sensed the presence of the Lord even as a young girl. Walking with God had been a priority for her. She had been part of the charismatic movement. So had her husband. In their spare time they had served as volunteer leaders in that community. After they moved to the Gulf, Martin got involved in a soccer ministry and Juliet helped him. They shared a love for youth.

But when they heard the ram's horn and walked into the service, they encountered something new. "I was totally under the anointing," Juliet says. She felt the Holy Spirit powerfully. That began ten years of fellowship and worship in this church, taking all the classes offered. "We grew up in the Lord," she says.

When they go back to India, they also continue to participate in Catholic retreats and find them enriching too.

Today Juliet works full time for the *shofar* church. Combining that and her volunteer service, her ministry is threefold: church mission administration, with a special focus on orphans and other children; soccer ministry; and labor camp ministry.

Prior to taking her church job, Juliet's days were filled with caring for the needs of her husband and three children, ministering to soccer players along with Martin, and preaching in one congregation that invited her occasionally.

That changed after Martin asked a Salvation Army officer, Major Holley, to give a talk to the soccer players. Here Major Holley got to know Juliet. Later, when the interchurch council was evaluating its makeup, one pastor observed, "We need a lady on the council."

"I have a lady," Major Holley said. He recommended Juliet.

As she served on the council, Juliet's skills became more widely known. Her large congregation invited her to apply for the position of director of missions.

"What is missions?" she wondered. When she learned that the job was administration, with an emphasis on child sponsorship, she felt right at home. Even before marriage, she had sponsored orphan children. "God saw what was there within me, and he put me in the right position in the church." This congregation sponsors four hundred children in India, Tanzania, and the Philippines.

Yet Juliet is not settled in her spirit. She has a deep desire to be doing ministry back in India. So does Martin. On the other hand, Juliet's mother lives in the UK and wants Juliet and Martin to move there.

"All the Goans are here in the UK. You can minister to them here," her mother pleads. "If you don't do it for yourselves, do it for your children."

God, where do you want us to go? Juliet asks. To appease her mother, she filed immigration paperwork. Because of Goa's special relationship with Portugal, Goans can enter Europe fairly easily. After Juliet filed, her Portuguese identity card came through quickly, somewhat to her dismay. "The more I tried to delay it, the faster it came," she grimaces. (Filing immigration papers leaves a sour taste in her mouth. Once she tried to immigrate to Australia, and paid a lot to an agent, but that unscrupulous scoundrel absconded with the funds. Now she has invested a lot in possible immigration to Europe.)

Voices clamor in her head. "Let's go for a time, to learn more so we can serve better," Martin says. "Let's not push away the opportunity."

"What are you doing about your papers?" her mother wonders.

"If the door opens for God to work, let's not close it down," Martin counsels.

"OK, I'm doing, I'm doing," Juliet mutters. "But really my heart is not there," she adds.

Meanwhile, the couple continue to pour love into the migrant Indian soccer players. Besides providing boys and young men with a wholesome outlet for their energies, soccer can also help them focus, aim for goals, learn teamwork, and discipline themselves. It can provide them with a framework for a more purposeful, well-rounded, and rewarding life. As such it makes a significant contribution to the community. It is also a good place to share the love of God in Jesus, and Martin and Juliet do that regularly.

They also minister in labor camps, where the poorest migrants live in the starkest conditions. Recently they were invited into a Hindi-speaking camp. Although that is not their mother tongue, they know how to speak it because it is India's major language. Later Martin and Juliet brought some of the Hindi-speakers to an evangelistic conference at the church. Many committed their lives to Christ.

They continue to seek invitations into camps, and minister where they are welcome. They also sponsor a group of prayer supporters who meet every Thursday to study the Bible. Some of them now join Martin and Juliet in ministry in the labor camps.

Who is Juliet's favorite Bible character? Esther, who fasted and prayed for her people. "Esther's life shows that the impossible can be made possible."

Like Charis, Juliet was discipled and trained after she arrived in the Middle East. Also like Charis and her husband, Ellis, Juliet and Martin form a team. Together they witness and then mentor younger Christians, helping them grow toward maturity.

I CHOOSE TO FORGIVE EVERY DAY

"I love this country," Charis says. "I love the people. But the workplace is hard." Work habits seem very casual. Local nurses may come to work, then sit down and drink tea, then work for thirty minutes, then sit and talk again. They leave jobs unfinished and expect the expatriate nurses to do the work. But if an expatriate makes a mistake, they come down hard on her.

Why is this? Many local nurses have Filipina maids in their homes. It is hard for them to shift their thinking so as to view a Filipina as a professional colleague. Sometimes they make mean jokes.

"When you are being taken advantage of, something hurts you inside," Charis says. "But I choose to forgive, to drop it, not to hold a grudge. I have to choose every day to forgive and not be offended."

Over the years, her fellow nurses have seen the blessing of God on her. "You are a Filipina, but you live in a house as nice as ours. You travel to places we've never been. You bring us gifts when you return, but we never bring you gifts." They draw a conclusion. "Your God is different."

When Charis arrived in the Middle East, she was a baby Christian. Today she is a mature trainer who has discipled many. Yet, in spite of her heavy ministry responsibilities, she always has held a job in the secular world. This has helped her know her context. Her work on the ward has kept her down-to-earth. It has rooted her in hard realities. Inevitably this has enriched her mentoring.

During her breaks, Charis sometimes reads the Bible. Her colleagues see that. One of the most difficult nurses—a woman who fights with everybody—recently asked Charis, "Can you get me a Bible in English that I can understand?"

Charis comments, "Second Corinthians says your life is like a letter that unbelievers are reading daily. I may not be able to read the Bible to my colleagues, but I *am* the Bible to them."

Bible Study Discussion Guide

1. Charis says, "I focus on the best." That means sidelining some other good things. What are you called to focus on? What should you sideline?

2. Charis and Ellis set goals for witness, for multiplying worship groups, and for discipling individuals. What kinds of goals could you set?

3. What kinds of help or resources would you need in order to meet those goals?

4. How does Charis handle insults?

Read and discuss this text about
GROWING MATURE CHRISTIANS:
Ephesians 4:12–16

CHAPTER FIVE

The Witness

Before you join a congregation in the Victory Church denomination, you need three things: a Bible, a notebook, and a passport so that you are ready to go where the Lord sends. You cannot become a member until you have them, according to Abby.

She was twenty-three years old and a brand new RN. She had received some training at the Every Nation Leadership Institute run by the church. She had also done some short-term missions. Although India had tugged at her heart, one month in Bangladesh and India showed her that that part of the world was not her call.

Then the pastor made an announcement that would change her life. "We need nurses in the Arabian Gulf, because we are planting a church there. A new hospital has opened up, and there are jobs."

Abby posted a note on the church bulletin board: "Are there any nurses interested in going with me to the Arabian Gulf to help plant a church?"

Seven nurses responded. All eight were commissioned and went out together.

Abby differs from the women we have met in earlier chapters, like Chelsea, Ginger, and Charis. Abby's number one purpose for coming to this region was to be a witness to the Lord Jesus Christ. Among the migrant laborers are others like Abby. Back in the home countries, a variety of training programs aim to equip these sojourners for effective witness. Thoughtful people in the home churches know that hardly any of the citizens in the Gulf countries worship Jesus as Lord. So they commission people like Abby.

WE WANT ABBY

In Abby's new hospital, it wasn't long until patients and their families were requesting her by name. "We want Abby." One reason she was popular was because she enjoyed speaking Arabic and used it every day. When she first arrived, she didn't know the language at all. However, she enrolled in an Arabic language course sponsored by a network of churches. From that time up to the present—eighteen years—she has continued to practice reading and writing as well as speaking Arabic with those around her. "For me, learning the language was not really that difficult because of my love for the people," she says. The passion to communicate propelled her to study and practice until she could understand and share life fully.

Of course, Abby joined a local church. Here she became part of a small group, as well as a member of the worship team. Soon several small groups started reaching out together to people who worked in fast food restaurants like McDonald's. A team would go to the fast food crew's dorm and wait for the workers to come home. Then they would offer to do a casual Bible study.

For the restaurant workers, this was something new. It brightened their dreary routines and expanded their horizons. It was a chance to have some friendly personal attention. And it was free.

For the study leaders, it was a demanding ministry. The Bible study and related travel might run until 3:00 a.m. Most of them had day jobs and had to get up by 7:00.

However, Abby did not spend all her time hanging out with church people. Her fellow nurses and her patients are Arab Muslims. And she lives in a villa-house with three Iranian women. Although Iranians are not Arabs, Iran is so near that you can almost see it across the calm blue waters of the Gulf. These two peoples have mingled and mixed and traded and intermarried for millennia. There are many Iranian business families rooted in the Arab countries of the Gulf, and many Arabs whose families have lived for generations in Iran. Abby begins and ends her days in a homey setting with Iranian women. Here she has learned to appreciate the nuances of their food. She has also begun picking up their language. Now she speaks not only Arabic but also Farsi. She has travelled to Iran several times, and has been able to encourage Iranians who are committed to Jesus. She has long-term friendships with people there.

MOTHER-IN-LAW MAGIC

Inside the hospital, Abby's colleagues include not only local nurses but also some from other Middle Eastern and African countries. She finds opportunities to talk with them about God and Jesus.

Nabuli is a colleague from North Africa. One day she came to work totally downcast. Because of their previous conversations, Abby knew that she was on the verge of divorce.

"Are you OK? You don't look so good," Abby said.

"No, I'm not," Nabuli answered.

"Can I help you?"

"I wish you could. I wish there was something somebody could do."

"Well, I'm not married, so I can't give you any counsel. But is it OK if I pray for you? I don't have anything to give you except my God."

"Yes, OK," Nabuli said with a shrug.

Since there were closed-circuit TVs in every corner, they moved to a hidden area. There Abby prayed for Nabuli and her husband.

Later they went out for coffee at Starbucks in the mall. "Do you love your husband?" Abby asked.

"Yes," Nabuli nodded.

"So why do you want to let him go?"

"Because of my mother-in-law," Nabuli groaned. "She is doing some magic on me."

"There is nothing impossible with my God," Abby said. They prayed again.

Nevertheless, the very next day, Nabuli found herself headed for divorce court alongside her husband. But they got a late start. As a result, the court was closed by the time they arrived. That was on a Thursday. The court remained closed on Friday because that was the regular day of worship.

Meanwhile, Abby asked Nabuli, "Do you believe there is an enemy behind this tension between you and your husband?"

"Yes. It's my mother-in-law," Nabuli agreed.

Abby smothered a chuckle. "No, I mean a cosmic enemy, a spiritual enemy. I mean Satan. Because God instituted marriage. And Satan wants to tear down God's work."

"Ah, yes, that could be," Nabuli said thoughtfully.

"Do you want to fight this battle? Do you want to fight for your marriage?"

"Yes, if my husband will fight also."

"Then let's pray and believe."

That afternoon, the moment that Nabuli walked in the door of her home, her husband apologized. Nabuli opened her arms and hugged him warmly.

Since then, Abby has been a regular visitor in that home. "Abby, can you come over for dinner?" Nabuli invites. "But be aware," she adds, "my husband doesn't know that you know about our situation." For his part, Nabuli's husband enjoys talking with Abby, and expresses his appreciation for her in general. "Why are you working in the hospital? You should work in sales. You have very good communication," he tells her.

Nabuli also invited Abby to her daughter's first birthday party. When she introduced Abby to the assembled guests, she said, "This is my best friend."

One day Abby offered to drive Nabuli home, even though it was a long distance. During the drive, Abby played a French worship CD. French is a common language in Nabuli's home country.

"Your song makes me cry, it is so beautiful," Nabuli said.

"Yes, it is," Abby said with a smile.

"But you worship *Isa,* right?" Nabuli reflected. (*Isa* is the Arabic name for Jesus.)

"Yes."

"And this song talks about him, right?"

"Yes, that he is great, that he cares about you and me, that he deserves glory."

Soon Abby will ask Nabuli if they can study Old Testament prophets together. Many of these are shared by Jews, Christians, and Muslims. But in Abby's study they will trace the prophecies that lead to Christ.

INTENTIONAL AND NATURAL

There was a period when Abby worked as a teacher in a preschool. Fatima was a teacher there too. She was from Algeria. "So what do you do for fun?" Fatima asked Abby one day. "What are your recreations? I have friends, but sometimes they are not real friends in this land."

"Oh, you can find friends here," Abby assured her.

"Yes, that's why I'm glad to see you. When I first met you, I knew that you would be my friend."

But Fatima would not help children when they had to go to the bathroom. "I'm a teacher. I wouldn't assist a child in the toilet. You are a teacher. Why would you?" she asked Abby.

"Well, if it's my child and the nanny is not there, why wouldn't I?" Abby answered.

Later Fatima said, "I guess I'm kind of a bad person. I love the kids but I can't go beyond my job description."

"Well, I don't just serve the kids," Abby said. "When I do this, I do it for my God."

Then they discussed yoga and meditation.

"I meditate, too," Abby said.

"How?"

"I read our holy book. Then I pray personally. Then I stop and ask my God, 'What are you saying?' Today my reading was 'Taste and see that the Lord is good.'"

Abby believes in being intentional. She looks for opportunities to talk about the Lord. As a practical step, she always gets her colleagues' phone numbers, as well as those of people she meets on the street. Yet it is not so much a matter of being intentional, she says, but being natural, being who you really are in your relationship with God. "It's the love of God that propels us. That is what makes me call them, or go to coffee, or go to the beach with them. When you're filled with the love of God, you don't have to struggle to be intentional. Jesus was himself. He slept when he needed to sleep. He ate when he needed to eat. And his work got done." She wants to leave a mark wherever she is from morning to night. But she is not stressed about this. People often tell her, "There's something in you. I can't figure out what it is." Some colleagues take the initiative to keep in touch with her even if they move on to other jobs.

From the very beginning, even before she set foot on these sands, she determined to shine as a light. Her first job interview was over the phone with a Syrian representative for a local company. "How come it's taking a long time for you to come over?" he protested. "You know in the Philippines all you do is go and pay something extra and you will make the papers move fast."

"Sir," she answered, "Although everybody is doing it, I will not. If you do not want me, that's the way it will have to be."

Since then, he has praised her publicly for her honesty, "even though she made me wait."

WITNESS ON THE JOB

Like Abby, Emma is a woman who witnesses when she has the opportunity. Emma came to the Gulf with two motives. She needed to make money, but she also hoped to be a light for the Lord. This is not easy in her workplace, where there is pressure to convert to Islam. Nevertheless, she has learned to use the situation for good.

Emma's boss leads the company prayers every day, in the morning, at noon, in the afternoon, and in the evening. Most of the Filipino men who work there have converted to Islam. They want to stay in the company.

"Oh, it's only *here* that I'm a Muslim," they confide to Emma. "When I go back to the Philippines, I will be a Catholic."

"It's not the same, it's a very big insult to God," she says.

"I have a family, so I need this job," they reply, grimacing.

"God will provide."

"When I return to the Philippines, I will go back to being a Christian, but for now I'm a Muslim," they say.

Still, they are hungry for the word of God. So Emma takes chances to share the goodness of God, to share testimonies of how God is providing. Coworkers often ask each other, "How are you getting along? How are you surviving?" It is a big witness when they see God's care for Emma.

"And even when I'm not saying anything to them, they see me always smiling. 'How can you smile like that?' they ask. I tell them the truth: 'God gives me peace.'"

Emma's boss, the man who leads the office prayers, periodically invites her to listen to the Quran. He also gives her religious books and videos.

In response, she shares her faith with him just as she does with her Filipino colleagues.

"We can go to God directly by means of Jesus, just as the Bible teaches," she tells him.

"No, the Bible is wrong," he says.

"My faith will not be changed, sir," she answers. "It's good that we both believe in one God. I know we have one God. But the difference is knowing God through Jesus. That is the most important thing. Because we human beings cannot go to God without knowing Jesus."

As well as speaking her witness, Emma has given her boss a leaflet entitled *Knowing God*.

THE MERCY OF GOD

Emma's boss means well. He takes the trouble to lead his workers in prayer because he sincerely wants them to know God. In actuality, Emma and her boss have a lot in common. Both believe that God is the creator, sustainer, and final judge of the world, and that he is all-powerful, all-wise, and merciful. Both believe God has put us into a world full of blessings. He has showered us with the gifts of nature and human community. He has sent us prophets and scriptures. Both Christians and Muslims believe that Jesus was born of a virgin, spoke the words of God, did miracles, was taken up into heaven, and will play a key role in the final judgment. Both want a more moral society, with strong families, modesty, laws that conform to God's word, and prayer and humble acknowledgement of God in public life. Of course Muslim-majority societies are a long way from this goal, just as so-called Christian societies are a long way from living out Jesus' teachings.

But there are glimpses of the happy, virtuous society that Muslims desire. Take the country of Oman, located at the southern tip of the Gulf. Here blue, blue sea meets razor-ridged brown crags, with gaps for small coastal towns. Gray-green sagebrush-like tufts dot the hills that climb to ten thousand feet. But with two thousand miles of coastline, the nation is oriented outward. Oman once ruled an Indian Ocean empire. Even today, there are reminders of that empire in the round castle towers that stand erect against the skyline—turrets constructed by Omanians, Portuguese, and Iranians.

At the national university, young women in black robes and flowered headscarves smile confidently as they cross paths with pleasant young men in simple white gowns and colored turbans. Sultan Qaboos University is named for the nation's ruler. This leader had the foresight to work toward a decentralized economy with small businesses and industries spread throughout the country, and to design a system that would employ local citizens more than foreigners.

The national mosque, also named for Sultan Qaboos, is a grand structure with pleasing proportions in marble and sandstone. Seemingly endless pointed arches recede down the vistas, spiraling out from the great center hall with its blue-domed ceiling and massive chandelier. Along one corridor, angular desert motifs are displayed on the walls. Here red color predominates. Along another corridor are designs from the Mughal period, with curves and flowerlike scrolls. Here blue predominates. This magnificent mosque calls Omanis to thank God for his mercies.

"Yes!" Emma and Abby would agree. "But the mercies of God are so much more." In Jesus, God came close to show us what he is like. In his death on the cross, God entered into human suffering profoundly. In his resurrection, he broke the boundaries of death and let loose power for a new level of living.

Muslims deny this. How could God die? How is it possible?

"Allahu akbar!" Abby and Emma would respond, echoing the daily cry, "God is great!" God can do anything. Who are we to tell him there is something he cannot do? If God chooses to go through death, can he not do so? God is greater than death. That is why Jesus burst out alive.

This is the true mercy of God—not only to create the universe, hold it together, and bring history to its final conclusion, not only to manifest wisdom and power and righteousness, not only to send us prophets and scriptures, but most of all to come close to us, enter into our pain, and explode out the other side of death.

Across the Middle East, migrant women like Emma and Abby testify to such a God, even when they work in humble jobs. Before eating, nannies pray. They sing when they iron. They play Christian music that their employers enjoy. They say, "Sir, I am praying for you." "Ma'am, God must have blessed you. May I thank God for you?" They request, "Sir, I need time off to worship." They tell their employers what their pastor preached. They watch Christian videos. Arab women regularly ask such maids for prayer, because when the maids pray, God answers.

IF I LOSE SIGHT OF THE CROSS

It has been eighteen years since Abby first landed in the Middle East. Since then, the seven nurses who arrived with her have returned home. Abby has stayed because she feels that God still is calling her here.

Worship music helps. "I write songs," she says. "Worship is my lifeline. If worship was taken away, I don't know what I would do. But worship is not about the songs you sing. It's about the heart that connects with the one who has loved you so much."

She likes any song that speaks about the magnificence of God, like "Indescribable" or "Holy is the Lord" by Chris Tomlin. She loves the line, "It's rising up all around / It's the anthem of the Lord's renown." Her own songs emphasize the nations coming to God, or relationship with God, or gratefulness. "To make him famous is why we live," she says.

Her favorite Bible text is Galatians 2:20: "I am crucified with Christ. Nevertheless I live. Yet not I, but Christ lives in me, and the life that I now live in the flesh I live by faith in the Son of God, who loved me and gave himself for me."

She comments, "Every day I have to be dead to self and alive to Christ. I have to be ready to go wherever he wants me to go. True, there are days when my flesh would want to resurrect. But I have to kill it. I'm dead. I'm dead. In Philippians 3:7,8, the Apostle Paul says everything is rubbish compared to this relationship I have with Christ. There's nothing else like it. I still celebrate every day. I always want to be reminded of my first love. Every day I say, 'Lord, take me back to the cross. Because if I lose sight of the cross, I lose everything.'"

David and Paul are Abby's favorite Bible role models, because they demonstrated leadership. She also admires Ruth, because she let go of her own identity and chose to worship the same God as Naomi.

Abby's father was a Jehovah's Witness. He died when she was fourteen years old. A few years later, when she started college, the whole family moved from their traditional home in Tarlac to Manila. Abby's grandmother was a believing Christian who had prayed for Abby fervently all through her growing-up years. Before Abby left for the Middle East, her grandmother and her mother both commissioned her. They laid their hands on her and prayed, and she received a powerful blessing.

Now, even in her field of service, Abby continues to attend training programs, such as one called Kairos and another called *Al Maseera*. At this moment she thinks God is directing her toward North Africa. Recently she had a dream. She told a Moroccan friend about it. "I had a dream that suggests something is going on in North Africa." Then she asked, "Is something unusual happening?" Sure enough, her friend told her, new things were happening. Political upheaval was bubbling. Abby wonders, was God telling her something through this dream? Some of her new friends are from Algeria, Tunisia, and Morocco, all North African countries. She is planning to do a study of the Old Testament prophets with two of them.

CAN YOU BUY MY WASHING MACHINE?

"Why do you always say *your* God? Isn't he *our* God?"

Abby was moving from one house to another. A man had come to buy some of her extra things. In the course of conversation, this question popped up.

"My God is different. He is almost like a father," Abby answered. "I don't have a dad anymore, but my God is very personal. He listens to me, and he cares. Just this morning I was praying, 'Can somebody come and buy this stuff and carry it away?' And then you came. You are an answer to prayer because you bought my fridge and my AC and you are going to carry them away!"

"I'm an answer to prayer?"

"Yes," smiled this woman of faith, who always takes advantage of opportunities. "And can you buy my washing machine too?"

Bible Study Discussion Guide

1. How important was speaking the language for Abby's friendship and witness? What made it easier for her to learn? How long did she study?

2. Abby is "intentional" and "natural" in witness. Give examples. How could you be more "intentional" and "natural" in witness?

3. When Abby and Emma explain the gospel to Muslims, what points do they emphasize?

4. "Worship is my lifeline. . . . To make him famous is why we live," Abby says. It's easy to forget that. How can you make this more central in your own life?

Read and discuss these texts about
WITNESS TO JESUS:
Matthew 28:18–20 and Galatians 2:20

CHAPTER SIX

The Giver

I'm sorry, I'm sorry. Don't tell my wife," the middle-aged man said to Melissa, backing up.

In order to help support her little daughter in the Philippines, Melissa had taken a job as a housemaid and nanny for a family with five children. Late one night, someone knocked on her bedroom door. When she opened it, her fifty-two-year-old employer started to push his way in.

She shoved at the door to shut it. He wrenched it back open, grabbed her, and manhandled her toward the bed. Fighting, struggling, and finally wriggling out of his clutches, she slipped from the room and ran down the corridor to the kitchen. There she snatched up a knife and whirled to face him.

At that point he held up his hands, apologized, and begged her not to tell his wife.

Yet a few months later the son of the house tried the same thing. Since there was no lock on her room, Melissa got into the habit of blocking the door with a table and chair and even the bed before she fell asleep. Still, the stress wore on her. Eventually she couldn't deal with it.

"I can't work in your house anymore," she told the wife.

"Oh, please—we'd like you to continue," the wife said.

"No, I'm sorry. I need to be released," Melissa insisted. She packed her things, and they reluctantly returned her to the Arab employment agency through which she had been hired.

For her next posting Melissa was assigned to a family with two children. The wife turned out to be pregnant and bad-tempered. She threw things at Melissa and slapped her. Once the children spit on Melissa and taunted, "You know, our last nanny, she jumped out the window and ran away."

Here, in contrast to her previous placement, Melissa was locked in her room at night, whether she wanted it or not. She was not free to go to church either. When she had first arrived, all her things had been inspected. Among them was a Christian book and an *Our Daily Bread* Bible study guide. The man of the house had grimaced at these and remonstrated, "There is no God but Allah."

Yet one day this boss also tried to assault her sexually. It happened in the kitchen. Melissa grabbed a knife and pointed it at her own neck. "If you go through with this, I will kill myself," she warned.

"OK, OK, I will not do it anymore," he said, relenting.

In December of that year he went on the *haj,* the holy pilgrimage to Mecca. However, in February he attacked her again. As a reinforcement he enlisted the help of a friend to watch the door and warn them if the wife was coming. He also locked the kids' door. Nevertheless, once again Melissa managed to fend him off.

This time she told his wife about it.

"I don't believe you," the wife said. She picked up the phone and called her husband.

"This Filipina is making trouble," he shouted over the phone when he heard what Melissa had said. "I'll come right home and take care of the problem."

As soon as the wife hung up the phone, she turned around and began beating Melissa. When the husband arrived, he joined in the assault, punching and slapping her. Then he heated a spoon and held it against the side of Melissa's face until she bled.

Eventually they let go of her. Melissa slipped to the refrigerator and got out a frozen bottle to hold against the burn. Then she overheard them saying, "Let's finish this. Let's kill her."

Domestic abuse of household help is so common that one prominent Filipino pastor in the Gulf advises women not to take these jobs if they have any other alternatives. "Stay home, even if you earn less," he counsels.

What can a woman like Melissa do?

WHO WILL HELP?

Auntie Faith has lived in the Arabian Gulf for thirty-five years. It was here that she came to know Jesus as Lord in a personal way. Here she has grown as a disciple. And it is here that she exercises her gifts in giving, serving, advocating, and networking to help many, including women like Melissa. The city government recognized Auntie Faith with a special award for humanitarian service in 2008. The national police have also commemorated her contributions.

Unfortunately there are many women like Melissa. Some factors that contribute to their suffering are systemic. These abuses must be addressed on a large, community-wide scale, rather than just case by case. Auntie Faith serves in both large and small arenas, pursuing justice as well as extending mercy.

"I was born with a heart that loves people," Faith says. Schooled by Catholic nuns in Cagayan, in the province of Isabela in the Philippines, Faith began going on missions with them when she was eight years old. She helped in a small church store, setting up inventory and selling. She went with the sisters to visit sick people in the hospital, and even accompanied them on trips into the mountains. "I never cared what color people were. And my love for others grew with my age. As I got older I became very involved with helping activities."

Academically, Faith did well, earning an MA in English and psychology, as well as a teaching degree. Yet because she was the oldest of eleven children, and because their father died when he was only forty-eight, Faith spent all her money trying to help her mother.

Beyond money, there was another problem. Her mother did not like her boyfriend.

"Maybe if I get you pregnant she will allow us to marry," he urged.

She did get pregnant, but her mother's attitudes didn't change, and in the end Faith didn't marry the man. So she became a single mom at age thirty-three. The nuns gave her shelter in an institution for unwed mothers, and later provided a home for her child there.

One of Faith's students was also a single mother. Her father worked in the embassy in Iran. "Your professor Faith should come out here," the father said. "She could earn a lot and provide a better life for her son." That is how Faith arrived in the Middle East.

In Iran, Faith met John, who was a British specialist in business contracts. When they first were introduced, John was engaged to a woman back home. During the months that followed, John and his fiancée broke their engagement, then renewed it. Meanwhile, life in Iran was exploding. One war followed another. Eventually, because of the wars and the political climate, John was required to leave.

By now he and Faith had grown close.

John soon got a job in another country in the Arabian Gulf. He phoned Faith. "I'd like you to join me here."

Faith made him say what he meant. "Why do you want me to come?" she asked.

"I'd like to make a proposal. I'd like to marry you."

First things first, Faith thought. "Go home and talk to your fiancée," she said. "Work things out with her so that everything is clear."

He did. After that, Faith flew to England. Because there was less paperwork involved if they got married in England, that is what they did. Then they returned together to the Gulf.

SPIRITUAL BIRTH

In her new home, Faith had a housemaid who often sat with her friends under a palm tree during their free time, singing and reading.

"What are you all doing out there?" Faith asked.

"Praising the Lord, ma'am."

"What is that about?" Faith wondered. Although she had grown up in the church, she had never picked up a Bible.

"We've been born again, ma'am. Come and join us."

"No, thank you," Faith said. But because she loved people she let the group of housemaids keep meeting. And she kept watching. Sometimes she felt a bit uptight when the maids went in and out, in and out, because the door would swing and bang and swing and bang.

Unaware that the banging doors offended their employer, these housemaids kept praying for Faith. This continued for ten years. Today Faith credits the Filipino church in this major city to that group of housemaids. "And I just love this church," Faith says. "It has brought me a good life in Christ."

But first she passed through three crises. Her mother was ill in the US, and her father-in-law was ill in England. Faith flew to be with each of them. Then she received word that her son in the Philippines had experienced a collapsed lung, and was hanging between life and death.

Her son underwent a delicate operation. In the end, all three of her dear ones came through their crises. However, for Faith the cumulative scares were a wake-up call. "I think it's time for me to be devoted to God, to be faithful, to serve him," she concluded. In a small chapel in the hospital where her son lay in intensive care, she knelt down and prayed, "Beginning today and extending to the end of my life, I will go forward with you."

"I was now fifty-five years old," she recalls. "I needed to learn the Christian faith faster than the average person." Back in the Middle East she got involved in a weekly Christian group, but that was not enough. A Chinese woman invited her to another set of women's Bible studies. Retreat speakers taught her more. Then she was invited to help with children's and women's ministries.

Today she attends both a Filipino church and an international church, and builds bridges between them to maximize benefits. When the Filipino church had fewer than forty members, they got teaching and preaching from the larger church. As they grew, it made sense to form a separate fellowship. This gave them increased opportunities to express their gifts with culturally appropriate nuances. Regardless of the organizational arrangements, Faith has journeyed with her brothers and sisters across the whole spectrum.

THE JOY OF JESUS

"I love sharing the word of God," Faith says. Even with taxi drivers she talks about Jesus. Many respond positively.

"At the moment I might not become a born-again," said one driver, "but I will remember everything you said to me, and who knows what might happen someday?"

In Faith's home the family laundry is washed by the maids, but she sends the ironing out. For thirteen years a Pakistani man named Mahadeen came to get the clothes, and later returned them freshly ironed. For thirteen years she invited him into her kitchen and explained to him who Jesus is.

One day a new man came to pick up the laundry.

"Where's Mahadeen?" Faith asked.

"Madam, he had a stroke."

"How is he?"

"He's in the hospital."

"If you see him, send him my love."

"You can visit him also, madam."

So Faith went to the hospital and found Mahadeen's room. When he saw her, he cried. He beckoned for her to come near him, and when she was close, he whispered, "I love Jesus."

"It took you thirteen years!" she said, but she smiled.

He shook his head. "You don't know what's been in my heart these thirteen years."

Later he was taken home to Pakistan. But the last time she saw him, Mahadeen gave her a victory sign.

THE JOY OF GIVING

"I love giving," Faith says. "I believe in giving." She repeats that, with emphasis. "*I believe in giving. It's* a special gift from God. When I accepted the Lord I said, 'Strip me of everything that once upon a time I loved in a worldly way.' And I have received the gift of giving."

It is not always material things, she adds. "You can give your time, your care." Faith sometimes offers cooking or babysitting to people who are sick. On Fridays, the day of worship, she prepares little packets with a bit of money to give to children who have nothing. Now other people give her supplies of things that can be given out to others.

One Friday Faith saw five new children streaming through the church. She struck up a conversation with their mother, and soon discovered that they were in dire need.

"I have all these children, and my husband is in prison because a check bounced," the harried mother disclosed. Her husband was a ship captain. He was well paid. But somehow their financial management had unraveled.

Faith gave the woman $100, as well as ten *dirhams* to buy a cake in the church basement so that they would have something to eat immediately. And she referred the woman to the pastor.

The next week, the woman came up to her. "Thank you. The pastor helped me. When my husband leaves the prison, he'll attend church with us." Still later the woman phoned

Faith, and asked, "May I come visit you? The children have made you a card."

Faith comments, "You have to be observant. Otherwise you may not notice needy people."

Sometimes what people need is prayer and encouragement, she notes. One Friday while Faith was supervising the ushers, an American wearing a long dress and a beautiful head covering walked up. "I'm Peggy," she said.

"The pastor prayed for you this morning, didn't he?" Faith asked.

"Yes, I have a cancer of the blood."

"Oh, I'm sorry. But I did pray for you."

"Thank you," Peggy said, and tears filled her eyes.

"Just this morning, I asked the Lord for someone to pray for. And here you are," Faith continued.

"Auntie Faith, I don't want to leave this earth," Peggy said.

"No, God is just showing you something in your life that will cause you to keep talking to him. The Lord will make you suffer a little bit now so that you will talk to him. One day you will be surprised that you are up and doing things that you used to do."

Faith and Peggy stopped and prayed together right there.

The next day Peggy phoned. "Auntie Faith, this morning I woke up so encouraged."

"You know what, Peggy? I have a special chair for Jesus. I set it facing me. While praying, I talk to him as though he was sitting right there. 'Come on Jesus. Talk to me,' I say. It's just like when you have a friend visiting. Why don't you try that?"

"OK, I will."

Overall, "the church is the right place for lonely people to come," Auntie Faith believes. "The church will not show you a bad life. There is always Jesus there. And if the time comes that you are hungry, go to a church. The church will feed you."

She smiles as she remembers Cherie, who is a member of her Bible study group. When Cherie first came to the Middle East, "she did a lot of crazy things. She slept with various men. She found herself in terrible fixes. One day someone shared the gospel with her and brought her to the Bible study. Today she lives beautifully with the Lord. There are lots of stories like this in our Filipino Bible study group," Faith says. "They are even thankful for their troubles here, because the difficulties of our life in the Middle East have made them run to the Lord."

SHELTER ME

Like stray cats, the runaway maids perch everywhere in the section of the embassy where they are allowed—on chairs and tables, on the floor, on the stairs. Some talk, but many are watchful. If greeted, their eyes light up and they respond. For such needy women, volunteers like Faith make an enormous difference.

There were three hundred maids living in the Philippine embassy when I visited, and four hundred in the Ethiopian embassy. There were Ghanaians taking refuge in the South African embassy because they had no embassy of their own. Hundreds more took shelter in the Sri Lankan and Nepali embassies. Technically these shelters are not approved by the governments. "We have government deportation centers for these women," officials say. Still, the shelters are tolerated.

An embassy is a regular working office, not originally equipped to be a shelter. The most it can offer is a bare floor space (after the day's working desks have been pushed aside) where the maids can roll out mats and sleep shoulder to shoulder, flotsam and jetsam washed up on an alien shore. In the daytime the maids crowd together in a waiting room. In the evenings they can use a TV, but no internet is available. The sound must be kept low. I saw one small laptop on which a few maids were watching a video. I didn't see anyone using a cell phone. There are two shelves of books and a sewing machine. Using this, women have designed and sewed dresses for in-house fashion shows.

Many of the women have long, thick, black pony tails. They wear what appear to be clean if uninspired shirts and pants, and there are no offensive body odors. How do they keep clean? There are five bathrooms in this building, and three hundred women, plus embassy staff and clients. Somehow they make it work.

One refugee, a Bible study leader, suffered from a cold. She had been trying to give money to a delivery man so he would buy cold medicine for her at a pharmacy. But he would not take the money. He did not want to get involved. A church conducts a medical mission to the women in this embassy once a month. Until then, the cold will go untreated.

NINA

Why do women come to such a crowded place? Maids run away because they are hit or yelled at, or because like Melissa they are sexually harassed or even raped, or because they are not paid.

When Nina arrived at the embassy, medical examination revealed profound abuse. As it turned out, she had reaped the results of her employers' spiraling frustrations with their own lives. The man of the house had had a wretched day at the office. He came home and took out his anger on his wife. She was hurt and furious. Then, when Nina stooped to pick up the baby, her feet tangled in her long skirt. She fell with the baby in her arms.

As Nina went down, she twisted so that it was her body that took the fall rather than the baby's. Nevertheless, her mistress exploded. Already in a rage, and with no other outlet, the woman attacked Nina. When Nina arrived at the embassy, her hands were completely burnt from bleach. Furthermore, her mistress had held Nina down and shoved hot chili peppers up her vagina. She had also cut Nina with a knife.

Nina is one of the few runaways with evidence for a clear strong case against her employer. Other maids may run away if they are not paid for months. When they file a case against their employer while they are sheltering in the embassy, sometimes the delayed salary will arrive. This is because the employer cannot legally apply for another maid if there is a case outstanding against him. On the other hand, sometimes an employer will make a preemptive strike and file a case against a maid before she can file, even against a woman he has raped.

ALMA

One embassy staffer specializes in the cases of maids who leave during the first hundred days of their employment. Some maids run away because they are homesick. An employer is supposed to pay for a maid's return ticket. However, if the maid has worked just a short time, or has left under a cloud, an exasperated or vengeful employer may refuse to sign an exit visa form. Then the maid hangs in limbo.

Forty-year-old Alma is a tailor. She holds a degree from a vocational training institute where she studied for two years after completing high school. Although she is a Muslim from Davao, she worked in a sweatshop in Manila where she sewed and finished one hundred T-shirts per day. This piece work fluctuated, however. Alma did not have enough money to help her two children, who are now nineteen and twenty years old, get established as young adults.

In the embassy, Alma was sitting by herself with a sad face and a few tears in the corners of her eyes. Most of the maids in the room were younger, and some were bouncy, flitting around. Alma has been in the Gulf for only four months, working not as a tailor but as a maid. But she was too homesick to continue. She left her position. Now she is charged with "absconding" and her employer refuses to provide an endorsement for her exit visa. She has been in the shelter for twenty-seven days. She is too sad to envision any hopeful future.

The government does give the embassies a certain amount of money each month. With this they can buy tickets for some maids, if they are legally free to depart. Other tickets are bought by the Salvation Army or other private donors, or by the maids themselves. Some maids stay confined here for a long time.

SARAH AND ESTELA

Ironically, many maids are not adequately prepared for the work they will do, as Chelsea noted in chapter 1. Not only do they not speak their employer's language, Arabic, but some do not even know how to do housework.

Sarah found this out the hard way. A British Christian who lives in the Gulf, Sarah had a new maid named Estela. One afternoon Sarah was going out. Before she left, she described the afternoon's tasks to Estela, showing her the cleaning ingredients and explaining how each was to be used.

When Sarah returned home later in the day, she walked in to find Estela spraying the TV screen with detergent.

Sarah screamed.

Estela cowered and raised her arm to ward off a blow.

"No, no. Don't worry. It's all right," Sarah said. "Just get water and wipe it very gently, like this."

After finishing that task, Estela began dusting the furniture. This she did with vigor. A picture flew off the wall and fell to the floor. The glass broke. Estela dissolved in tears. Sarah found herself consoling the maid once again. Throughout the afternoon the fiasco continued, and Sarah saw that the faults in employer-employee relations in the Gulf are not all on one side.

SUSTAINABLE SOLUTIONS

"Do you have any scraps for me today?" Helen asked with a smile.

We had parked near a small strip of shops near the embassy. All were tailor shops owned by Indians. A few months ago Helen had visited this strip, introduced herself, and described the plight of the women taking shelter in the embassy just a couple of blocks away. She intended to help the women create craft articles for sale, Helen explained. Would the tailors be willing to set aside fabric scraps rather than throwing them out? She would come to collect the scraps every week.

Today, as we strolled down the corridor, one tailor hefted up two bags that were almost too big to carry, and promised more. Another said he would provide scraps the following week. A third, who was new, looked like he would like to get in on the good work in the future. But others grimaced and drew back.

At the end of the aisle we stopped at a samosa shop to buy sixty small vegetable pastries. These would complement Helen's tin of Danish cookies. She has been in the country just six months and confesses that she is not good at learning languages. Yet she is willing to reach out and develop new relationships that not only help the women shut up in the embassies but also enable local people to participate in worthy projects that serve others. Soliciting scraps, Helen also saves money and helps the environment.

Besides the tailors, another supplier is a local woman whom Helen met at a recycling fair. This woman regularly gives Helen used plastic bags to be employed in crafts. For a long time the woman thought Helen's project was recycling. Now she knows the true purpose, but continues to donate bags.

With these plastic bags, the detained women have made sturdy small area rugs, similar to rag rugs. Helen's sales network is rudimentary. The rugs and other crafts are sold at informal group bazaars. When Helen's son visited at Christmas, he took some rugs home to the UK, and he and his friends have been selling them at folk markets. So far the women have earned $400 from their rugs. Half the proceeds go to the individual rugmakers, and half to the general fund to capitalize more projects. Helen tries to observe what combinations of colors will sell and instructs the women accordingly. She also switches to a new product when they have made a quantity sufficient for her market contacts.

I observed the making of Christmas wreaths, a fun and potentially economically productive group activity. Helen had downloaded pictures of various artificial Christmas wreaths from the internet and passed those around. Since Filipinos make and hang Christmas stars rather than wreaths, and since some of the women were Muslims with no Christmas tradition, the making of wreaths was a new kind of project. Thirty to forty women gathered around two portable tables or sat on the floor. In various natural groups, they cut, wound, pinned, glued, and sewed scraps of cloth around plastic hoops that Helen had picked up somewhere. Creativity blossomed.

"How about this? Or no, maybe these fabrics contrast better? Let's make a candle design. See, this can be the flame. And we can put little flowers here."

Some furrowed their brows in concentration. Others chattered constantly, dialoguing about their designs in a continual loop of conversation.

"Thanks for reminding me about that project," Helen's husband had said when I talked to him earlier in the day. "As I drive home, I'm supposed to look for dead palm branches that have fallen on the ground. She wants to spray them with gold to add to the wreaths." (As it turned out, he forgot. But the women managed fine.)

"I WAS IN PRISON, AND YOU VISITED ME"

Women sit idle and hopeless not only in embassies but also in prisons. Some are behind bars because their employers have accused them of robbery, often for stealing money or jewelry.

Office girls have bounced checks or used fraudulent credit cards. Other women have stolen from supermarkets. Others are snared for working at unregistered part-time jobs or for living with their boyfriends, through this rarely concerns the police unless someone reports it. Formerly such accused persons would have been deported. Now they are imprisoned. They must be punished. They must pay for their crime.

Most of the prisoners are from the Philippines or Africa. A few are pregnant when they are arrested, and may give birth while in detention. If so, they keep their babies with them in the prison.

Juli had a husband, a son, and a daughter, and was pregnant with her third child. One day, she says, a Filipina approached her and asked her to carry a package to an address. "I'll pay you one thousand *dirhams*," the woman added.

"What is it?" Juli asked.

"A bag of sandwiches."

Juli opened the bag and looked in. Yes, it was sandwiches.

As she neared her destination, police stopped her. "What's in this bag?" they asked.

"Sandwiches."

When the police rummaged through the bag, however, they found drugs underneath the food.

At first Juli had her two young children with her in the prison. She fretted over this. "How can I expose my children to this jail life?" she groaned. "I want to send them to my husband so they will not witness all this. But now my husband is living with my younger sister, and I don't want my kids to see that."

Auntie Faith was visiting the jail that day and listened to Juli pour out her heart. "Pray," Faith advised, "and the Lord will give you your answer." Juli was a nominal Christian.

Yet when Faith returned some time later she discovered that Juli had become a Muslim. She had been promised that if she converted to Islam she would be freed.

However, that is not what happened. Although she became Muslim, Juli is still in prison. Her children have gone to be with her husband. Her sentence is twenty-five years for transporting drugs.

Christian women like Auntie Faith reach out to these incarcerated women. Visiting regularly, they bring toothpaste, clothes, shoes, makeup, and Bibles. For a while an American volunteer insisted on trying to start programs. "We must have yoga," or "We must have sewing," she would say. However, this caused problems because it annoyed the prison officials. Eventually the other volunteers were able to persuade her to adopt a more low-key approach.

Some prisoners know that there is a God, according to Auntie Faith, but they have never held a Bible. If prisoners want Scriptures, the volunteers make them available. Some lives are changed as the women read the Bibles. "When we come back on our next visit, they cry and say, 'Had I known how wonderful it is to know Jesus, I would have lived differently!'"

"Well, this is the time for you to do that now," Auntie Faith responds. "Because you suffered so much, the Lord who loves you said, 'I'm going to send you to a place where you can learn to know me and can experience the love of others.'"

One prisoner vowed, "Before I came here, I had never known people who give themselves as you give yourself for us.

When I leave this place, wherever I'm going I'm sure there will be a place like this, and I will serve there, devotedly visiting, giving, serving like you do."

Auntie Faith does get tired. Then she remembers that when Moses was tired God directed Aaron to hold up Moses' arms. A few years ago Faith started a prayer group with five people. Today it has seventy members. With them she praises and intercedes and enjoys the presence of God. They hold up her arms, like Aaron did with Moses.

What is her favorite Scripture text? "There are so many. John 3:16. Psalm 77. But especially Jesus saying, 'I will never leave you or forsake you'" (Heb 13:5).

WAKING UP BURNED

What about Melissa, who was beaten and burned on the cheek by her employers, then overheard them planning to kill her?

She was so weak from the beating that she couldn't run away. She simply prayed, "Lord, I commit myself to you. I'm ready to be with you. I commit my loved ones to you, especially my daughter." Then she passed out.

Just before she lost consciousness, she saw a light in front of her and heard a voice saying, "I will not take you now, because I have a purpose for your life."

Melissa woke up the next day in the hospital. It turned out that instead of killing Melissa, her employer's wife had transported her to the hospital. She claimed that Melissa had tried to commit suicide. But Melissa's wounds were not consistent with this story. A case was filed against the employers. The man tried to hide abroad for six months but was apprehended in the airport when he returned and jailed temporarily.

While the case continues, a migrant Christian who is a nurse has taken Melissa into her home as a maid and is discipling her.

This is the same kind of response that Auntie Faith has fostered during her long years of service in the Middle East. Life can be hard anywhere. Certainly that is true in the Gulf. In the middle of it all, women can practice mercy and work for justice.

Bible Study Discussion Guide

1. What are important aspects of giving, according to Faith? Think about your own giving. What factors do you consider?

2. How long does Faith wait before she starts witnessing to a person? What makes her witness gracious rather than intrusive?

3. Think about some people who have seen or heard your witness for years. Then think about the Pakistani laundryman who told Faith, "You don't know what's been in my heart these last thirteen years." Does that encourage you even though you don't see results?

4. Picture the runaway women who take sanctuary in embassies. How can you pray for them, and for those who minister to them? Be specific.

Read and discuss these texts about
GENEROSITY:
2 Corinthians 8:1–9 and 9:6–15, especially 9:8

CHAPTER SEVEN

The Pastor

Like butterflies, the saris swirl past—yellow, turquoise, lavender, rose, sea green—as women slip into the worship service of Praise God Ministry, an Indian Telugu church in the Arabian Gulf. Hundreds of women crowd into the front and down one side of the room. On the other side and across the back sit hundreds of men. There are also a few families sitting together.

"Even if nobody shows you any respect all week"—the pastor counsels the women, many of whom are poor housemaids—"when you come to church, you are princesses welcomed into the house of the King of kings and Lord of lords. So wear your very best saris. And if you have any gold, wear your gold!"

Indeed, gold does flash from ankles and bare toes and fingers and wrists and necks and ears as women bow in prayer on their mats. Diamonds sparkle in nose rings. Traditionally the bank of the poor, jewelry glows here to praise the Lord.

Five kinds of drums—some short, some tall, but all wider in the middle than at the ends—join one keyboard to create loud music. As in the traditional Hindu worship music known as *ragas*, melodic motifs repeat. But the topic here is worship to the Lord Jesus Christ. People stand and sway, and a sea of arms stretches up, hands clapping. In reverence many women draw their saris over their heads, but during the singing most of these fall back down. Rows of chairs extend all the way to the back of the big room. In front of them, an area about forty feet long is covered with mats. Here women sit cross-legged, their shoes stacked up against the wall, pair upon pair, to a height of three feet. Periodically an usher will squeeze these women closer in order to open up space for three or four more rows. Latecomers will have to sit on the edge of the platform itself.

Amid the harmonic vibrations and throbbing drumbeats and dizzying array of colors, women and men are reminded that they are made in the image of God, valued so much that God descended to the depths to die for them, and empowered because God in Christ rose to give them new life. Shoulder to shoulder, singing, swaying, raising hands, they see and feel that they are not alone. Worship creates a world, and it is a world these people truly need to inhabit. Many cannot attend every week. Their employers do not permit it. So whenever they can come, they arrive with thankfulness.

Three-fourths of them were born into Hindu families. Originally the church focused on the very poor. Now it is broadening as the Telugu working community diversifies. Pastor Indra's dream is "to see these downcast people enjoying the presence of the Lord and transformed like Christ. Christlikeness makes a lot of difference in society," she says.

WHO IS PASTOR INDRA?

Growing up in Hyderabad in India, Indra studied nursing. She was one of the youngest nurses brought into the operating theater in her area. Eventually she became a professor of nursing. Then, right in the prime of his life, her father died. As his oldest child, Indra felt a responsibility to help the family financially. So she took a job in Bahrain.

Indra's grandparents had been educated people. Her grandmother ran a language school where she taught Arabic, Farsi, and Urdu. When English-speaking missionaries arrived, Indra's grandparents translated for them. In so doing, they heard the gospel. After they gave their hearts to the Lord, in time they also gave significant property to the church. Indra's grandmother became a great prayer warrior.

But Christianity was just formal tradition for Indra. During worship services, she and her friends would position themselves where their parents could not see them so that they could sneak out. Indra was an active and fearless child, climbing trees like a monkey. (She is still high-energy today, intense and passionate.)

In Bahrain, Indra met Ram, the man who would become her husband. They dated for three years. He is in banking and finance and serves as chief financial officer for a very significant company. He is also Brahmin, a member of the highest caste.

When they married, although Indra was a Christian only in name, she pleaded, "Please don't make me worship idols."

"No, I will never force you. If you don't like something, you don't have to do it," he assured her.

Later, when Indra became an active Christian, Ram did not object, because he did not practice Hinduism actively himself.

They married across religious and caste lines, but both their families accepted and blessed the union. For the marriage ceremony, they returned home to India. Then they moved to Kuwait.

Soon Indra was pregnant.

With joy they welcomed a healthy son into the world.

GUNSHOTS!

One night when their son was just three months old, they were awakened out of a sound sleep at 3:00 a.m.

"Gunshots!" Ram recognized the thunder. They leaped from bed and peeked out the window. Ships were arrowing into the harbor. Above their heads, planes roared. It sounded like a war zone.

Ram grabbed the phone and dialed friends.

"You must be dreaming," their friends yawned.

But a few minutes later, Iraq Republican Guards were banging on their door and taking over their home. Carrying only the baby and a handbag, Indra crept out. Providentially, the purse contained her passport and some cash.

For eighteen days they lived as refugees in friends' houses, quivering from every kind of stress and fear and anxiety. They had been wealthy. "Now all I had for my three-month-old was one blanket." Pus still oozed from her abdomen because an infection had developed following her cesarean section delivery.

After two and a half weeks they got hold of a car and drove through Basra to Baghdad, then across the desert to Jordan, where they rushed into the Indian embassy. The embassy put them up in a hotel. For the next several days they filled out forms for illiterate refugees. Almost a hundred long-distance truck drivers were among those seeking their help.

Finally they found a spot on an Indian chartered plane. Although they felt safe once they landed in Bombay, they had no money. Eventually they would go on to the UK and then the US. Indra would endure three more surgeries to repair the damage of the cesarean delivery. In 1996 they would return to

Kuwait. But before that happened, her life would change from the inside out.

While they were living in Boston, Indra conceived their second child. When the fetus was three months along, doctors gave them very bad news. Tests indicated that the baby probably would be retarded. An abortion was advised.

"Would you please pray for me?" she begged some Indian Christian friends who were also living in Boston.

"You? Want prayer? You were never religious before," they teased. But they did indeed pray earnestly for Indra and her unborn baby.

One month later, tests showed a normal fetus. Today that son is sixteen years old. He is studying Advanced Placement courses in the American School of Kuwait and has received prestigious awards.

BAPTISM WITH GOLD

This experience turned Indra's attention toward God. Up to that point she had respected God, but the respect had been vague. Now, as she looked back on her life, she saw what a roller coaster it had been, with losses from war and then repeated surgeries. She sensed that some divine power had been at work. But she did not know how to connect with it.

As she gave attention to this, she began to have visions. They appeared to come directly from Jesus. "I used to see him as if he was walking into my room. He showed me his wounds," she recollects.

She would shake her husband awake. "What's happening to me?"

"Oh, you love your god, so maybe he's coming to you," Ram would answer sleepily.

Even before the baby was born, Indra was experiencing these visions. Then she went into labor. Again the delivery was complicated. Inadvertently, a large piece of the placenta was left in the abdomen. For three weeks Indra bled profusely. Not detecting the problem, doctors insisted there was nothing wrong.

The dead tissue could have become toxic, but again God's hand intervened. Indra discharged the placenta piece naturally.

When she showed the tissue to her doctor, he was appalled. "I am so very sorry," he said. "If you want to go to court over this, you can."

Instead of going to court, Indra started going to church with a friend.

"I didn't like the speaking in tongues," she remembers. "But when the pastors preached the word of God, I liked it so much. I became addicted to the Word. Then I wanted to learn the Bible for myself, not just depend on pastors. I could see that illumination, that inspiration, in the Scripture. I saw connections between one part of Scripture and another. I began to read the Bible for two or three hours at a time, and every day there was something new. I wanted so much to know God."

Indra grew in her understanding and commitment, and prayed to receive Jesus Christ as Lord of her life. Then she wanted to be baptized.

"Yes, you are ready," the church discipleship coordinator said. "But you will need to put away your gold jewelry after you are baptized."

"What?!" For millennia when Indian families have managed to save any money, they have invested it in gold. Women wear this in the form of jewelry. It serves both economic and aesthetic ends. Gold enhances a woman's beauty and also indicates that she is a valued member of a stable family. The Arabian Gulf has been a prime source of gold for India.

However, the church where Indra worshipped was part of a conservative Pentecostal denomination. "Jesus put aside his splendor and became a lowly servant. When we go down into the waters of baptism, we follow him," the church leader explained to Indra.

She raised her eyebrows and snorted. "When Abraham's servant went to get Rebecca, he brought gold. The temple was decorated lavishly in gold. And what about heaven? Why do I have to remove a chain when there are *tons of gold* in heaven? *Tons of gold!*"

The church leaders knew Indra's conversion was real. Her spiritual insights were profound. So they sought permission from their denominational directors on this matter.

Permission was granted. "You are an exceptional case," it was decided. "We are giving you baptism *with* gold."

HOURS IN THE WORD

After they returned to the Gulf in 1996, Indra discovered "Pastor Jerry's church." Lighthouse Church is part of the National Evangelical Church of Kuwait. Its head pastor, greatly loved and respected, was an American named Jerry. Bethel Bible Class was a series that he taught. Although Indra developed asthma in the Kuwaiti dust, she attended the classes devotedly, coughing right through them because "learning about God is very precious." She memorized Scripture avidly. For eight years she took all the classes she could get.

After a class, she would review the material in her Bible and search for related texts. She began to meditate on the Word day and night. "God and I were conversing," she says. "I saw God's heart, mind, and emotions. I saw that we hurt his heart. I saw his love." Studying God's conversations with his children Abraham, Moses, Josiah, and so many others, she grieved for God's pain. "How can I make God's heart happy?" she wondered. "When you have a *guru,* you think about how to make your teacher happy, particularly if many people have hurt him. I wanted to hear, 'Well done, faithful servant.'"

Meanwhile, she was reaching out to friends and neighbors, beginning with a group of seven people. "Why don't we sit and pray?" she suggested. God answered all sorts of prayers, especially for healing. Before they prayed, she would give a fifteen-minute exhortation from the Word. "I didn't know much of the word of God, but I had a passion to read the Bible and meditate and understand God's heart. I wanted to give people the love of God. This was precious to me. I never thought I would be a pastor, but I spent hours in the Scripture, and learned that I was blessed to be a blessing."

One day, after she had talked about the Beatitudes from the text in Matthew 5, someone suggested, "Maybe you could speak to a larger group, to a church." That was a new idea, but she was willing to grow in that direction. Pastor Jerry saw her calling, and after eight years of classes and individual tutoring, he ordained Indra to the ministry. Her small groups multiplied into what is today a large church. This congregation is connected with Lighthouse Church as part of the National Evangelical Church of Kuwait.

Indra's husband, Ram, also discovered Jesus as Lord. The deciding moment happened while Indra was away from home, visiting overseas. Somebody invited Ram to hear an evangelistic speaker. He didn't want to go. "I'm so tired. I've had such a long day at the office," he muttered. Nevertheless, he agreed to go.

Just as he had expected, he was disappointed. He didn't like the evangelist's voice. He didn't like the shouting. So he closed his eyes.

Then the Holy Spirit came upon him, and Ram began speaking in tongues.

That night he phoned Indra overseas with great excitement. "Indra, Jesus is real! What the Bible says is real! What the preacher says is real!"

Indra comments, "For both of us, we didn't have mediators. We had only God touching us. My husband is a backbone to me. Poor man, he earns and I spend (for ministry). He has always modeled virtue and understood and supported me, especially when I went through many surgeries. He is more than a husband. He is also like a brother."

In turn, Ram says of Indra, "There is consistency between what she says and what people see her live."

ALL PEOPLES, TRIBES, KINDREDS, AND NATIONS

Coming through the front entrance of the National Evangelical Church of Kuwait compound, I climbed ten long curving cement steps. They constituted an area big enough to seat a small crowd. Within the compound, palm trees and other greenery were interspersed between buildings of varying shapes and sizes, two of them bookstores. A round, bright blue well-like structure five feet across served as an occasional baptistery.

In front of me an Indian congregation (different from Pastor Indra's) sat cross-legged, men on one side and women on the other, swaying to fast, loud drumbeats. Across the way, a more solemn Indian group celebrated Holy Communion in high Anglican fashion. To the left, a Filipino congregation praised God, led by a vibrant band and worship dancers. I encountered Chinese and African worshipping groups, youth playing soccer, and other youth rehearsing a choral piece. An hour later I watched all these groups stream out to make way for new ones who came flooding in.

How did this begin? More than a hundred years ago, a Dutch medical missionary removed the cataracts from a royal princess's eyes. In gratitude the ruler donated a few acres of land for a mission hospital and worship center. Now there are over 150 meetings every week in this compound. About thirty of these are part of Lighthouse Church, the original English-language congregation. Other groups here worship in other languages. However, in recent years Lighthouse itself has been planting fellowships in various languages. Indra's group is one of those. Counting all the extensions, at the time when we interviewed Indra about twenty thousand people were worshipping in Lighthouse services each week.

Several Gulf countries allow similar clusters of congregations (though Saudi Arabia does not). Often these churches are situated on land next to other non-Muslim houses of worship, Protestant, Catholic, and Orthodox, and sometimes also Hindu or Buddhist. Some compounds host bookstores or elementary schools. Additionally, hundreds of house churches vibrate throughout the region. Many are networked with the established churches.

According to *The Christian Church in Kuwait: Religious Freedom in the Gulf* by Andrew Thompson, Arabic-language congregations here are connected with the Coptic Church of Egypt, the Assyrian Church, the Armenian Church, the Greek Catholic Church, and the National Evangelical Church. Most Protestant bodies connect with the evangelical Synod of the Nile or the National Evangelical Synod of Syria and Lebanon, both members of the Middle East Council of Churches. Arab Christians in the Gulf are Egyptians, Lebanese, Palestinians, Jordanians, and a small number of local citizens.

Indian churches are numerous, especially those worshipping in Tamil, Telugu, or Malayalam languages. (Amazingly, among the eighty-four congregations that worship at the National Evangelical Center in Kuwait, *twenty-five* serve Indians from the state of Kerala alone.) Indian churches sponsor ministries for youth, children, and women, magazines, all-night prayer meetings, weekly services in labor camps, and numerous charity projects in India. "Thousands of men, women, and children worship God in at least five Indian languages. They serve their communities through education, health care, charity and simply by being good citizens under the laws of Kuwait," Thompson says (2010, 110).

Additionally, theological education programs with varying degrees of rigor have been set up by Indians, Filipinos, and others. Chelsea (chapter 1) graduated from a three-year course of study. Besides worship services and choirs, crisis responders and classes for children and adults, these churches-away-from-home also host programs as varied as Alpha courses or dynamic singles groups serving members from six continents. Most importantly, "Many people get saved. They think they come for money for their family, but they end up getting saved. They are hungry for something more, and they find it here."

TRAINING, OUTREACH, AND CELEBRATION

"Souls are my passion, along with integrity and honesty in the ministry," Indra says. "That's what I learned from Pastor Jerry. Speak the word of God. Truth is truth. Don't add or take out anything. God is holy. And what you are learning in the Christian fellowship has to apply outside."

Indra is tutoring two full-time pastoral associates. Combined with herself and her husband, this makes a pastoral team of four. Beyond this core group are a dozen people who are employed elsewhere but surround Indra as their *guru* and run to do the work of the church in their spare time. Driving, fulfilling errands, procuring supplies, serving guests, bringing Indra water before the service—they do whatever is necessary. A visiting speaker ended his platform time by telling the congregation she was their chosen leader and they could show their worship to God by submitting to her. She was their covering.

Every Wednesday Indra prepares her leaders. She starts with "cleansing stream evangelism," then discipleship, then teaching on leadership and theology. While still in training, these learners also go out to find seekers and bring them in. Three days per week the team does outreach, and Indra goes with them. They go house to house, one week to one area, the next week to another. Sometimes they distribute CDs so that people can hear the Word. They ask, "Do you have any need?

We'll pray for you. What can we do for you?" They expect the Holy Spirit to work in the lives of the people they meet.

During their training time each Wednesday, they go through the list of needs that people have expressed and pray for them. After all, they have assured people that they will do this, saying, "According to the book of Acts, God's people prayed, joined together, and took care of each other. That's what we do. So come to our church!"

Since construction laborers have no money to pay bus fares, the church offers free transport from the labor camps to the worship services. Twenty busses are in service. Sometimes the church also distributes rice or lentils to the laborers because these communities suffer from hardcore poverty.

Indra also gives pastoral care to the church youth, taking the initiative to raise questions when she sees a need. They relish somebody showing them attention and seem to take to heart what she says. Periodically the youth themselves will visit the labor camps. Like the adult outreach team, they will ask, "What do you need us to pray for?"

The annual celebration crowns it all. This is a gala explosion of food, song, dance, drama, drums, friendliness, and joy expressed by people who own little yet have been empowered to tap into their gifts to praise the Lord and serve the community. Once a year, usually early in December, they throw a huge party in the compound. Thousands show up. There is a home-cooked meal, small gifts, and original dramatic productions sparkling with songs, dances, costumes, and scenic backdrops all created by the members themselves. No outside talent is brought in. Indra wants the members to showcase their own gifts. Joy in the gospel and joy in the culture are woven together. Lots of DVDs are recorded and made available. Even the sheikh's daughter attended as an honored guest last year.

There are men's dances, women's dances, and children's dances. For months they work on the choreography, costumes, scenic backdrops, posters, and intricate steps. I watched women wearing their ordinary work pants and tops twirl through the practice of a dance that used fans. Less flowing, more vigorous and strong are the men's dances. They hint at martial arts. The tunes accompanying the dances are Indian worship songs.

For days before the event, women congregate in Indra's home kitchen to fashion sweets and prepare other foods. On the day itself, huge kettles on gas burners line her side yard. Here hundreds of kilos of spicy chicken simmer. Men cook the chicken because it is heavy labor.

"Three hundred sixty-five days a year you work for others," Indra says to her people. "One day you come and enjoy yourselves."

Through it all, Indra sees lives transformed. One of her assistants spent twelve years in prison. Another, the son of a prostitute, suffered from polio, but was healed and now is an active volunteer, faithful and reliable, a pillar of the church. Others have come from adulterous relationships.

Such relationships are common. Many of the laborers are on five-year contracts, and in order to save money they might not go home at all during that period. To avoid a promiscuous lifestyle and to experience some semblance of home, many a man will select a woman and say, "Come live with me. I'll pay your living expenses. You can send all your earnings straight home. When we go back, we'll separate; you return to your husband, and I'll return to my wife."

The need to repay debts propels women into these arrangements.

Indra will not baptize a couple who are living together but not married to each other. They have to separate. "But I can't tell them to separate without thinking about their financial needs. Previously pastors did not have as much understanding of life, but now we know more about family realities," she says. Sometimes she gets sewing machines for women. She would send them for skill training if she could. She tries to create jobs. She also seeks out existing jobs, regularly asking friends and acquaintances if they could hire someone, especially if she knows a job seeker with particular skills. "If these women could get sixty-five dollars more per month, they would not need to prostitute themselves," she laments.

Home leaves are encouraged today more than they were previously, because companies are coming to realize that these make laborers more productive. But many women have taken out loans and owe too much. They cannot even telephone their husbands because it is too expensive. Meanwhile, the children back home may buy motorbikes with the hard-earned money that is sent home, not understanding how their parents struggle and suffer. Teaching on family finances may be important at both ends of the migrant arc.

Yet, as they grow in Christ, many adulterous couples do separate. They kneel down and say, "These things we didn't know before. Nobody explained them to us. Now that you have taught us, our hearts want to follow."

Such believers are "like my right hand and my left," Indra says. "The old has passed, the new has come and has the character of Jesus. Now there are mighty men and women in my army.

Without their help, I could not do the ministry." Many are illiterate, but educated professional people are also joining the church, and together they are experiencing a passion for God.

OIL RUNNING DOWN THE HAIR

As the saris swirl and people scoot close together on the mats, Indra opens the worship service. Because they share the building with many other congregations, her time is limited.

The first two weeks of every month she focuses solely on the preaching of the Word. The third week includes anointing people with oil. The fourth week includes the bread and wine of Holy Communion.

"In the two-hour slot, I have to finish praise and worship, testimonies, prayers, and the word of God. What we do varies each week, depending on the Holy Spirit. I want to bring people to the cross. I don't want them to go away from God. God's presence should set them free. All week they are in bondage. The truth of the word of God will set them free. So we have freedom in worship, led by the Spirit."

Although the service is in the Telugu language, Indra looks for translators, because some participants come from other Indian groups. She uses PowerPoints during her sermons. Because many of her members are not literate, she also uses pictures on her laptop. She tries to "move God to their level" as she explains and applies the Word. The congregation listens attentively.

From the very beginning of her ministry Indra recorded her messages, so big cameras are present near the platform. She provides CDs of the worship service at cost. Many people are not permitted by their employers to come every Sunday. They want the CDs. Even those who have attended may want to hear the word of God repeated. While domestic employers sometimes object to the internet or even cell phones because they have heard of maids getting into trouble through these media, often they are willing to provide a CD or DVD player.

As she applies Scripture to her hearers' physical needs, Indra weaves teaching about health into her sermons: how to take care of our bodies; how to eat with good nutrition; maintaining hygiene, even in "houses so small you can hardly walk in the room"; avoiding gluttony and drunkenness; preventing common diseases; and forgiving others as a step to mental and physical health.

During the worship service on the third Friday of every month, Pastor Indra and her team offer personalized prayers, so valued by the powerless people in her congregation. In the closing half hour of the service, they pray for a thousand people individually. Six or seven pastoral assistants spread out across the front of the platform. Worshippers who want prayer create several long lines. Each line leads to an officiant who holds a pitcher or an animal horn filled with oil for anointing.

Gently a woman from the line will sink to her knees, facing a pastor, and slide her sari backward off her bowed head, revealing thick, wavy black hair parted in the middle and fastened at the nape with a barrette or white flowers, fresh or artificial. The pastor pours a dollop of oil where the hair meets the brow and murmurs a prayer for this sister. She may reach out and gently clasp the pastor's feet, as she might do in a similar Hindu rite, but an assistant will brush her hands away, because the pastors are not gods. "In the name of Jesus. Amen," the pastor says, and the woman lifts her eyes and glows.

She may hold out a cupped palm for more oil, which she will rub on a part of her body not open to view. She may bring a bottle for oil to give to a sick friend. She may whisper, "I have no child." Prayer focuses on that. Others ask for prayer for a visa or a job. Or they say, "I'm not well." Or "My daughter is getting married."

As the woman straightens to her feet, a laboring man shuffles forward, drops to his knees, and presents his bowed head. Whether his hair is springy and thick, or thin and graying, he waits humbly for anointing and the blessing of God to face another week of hard work.

In the migrant churches in the Arabian Gulf, managers and maids, executives and fitness coaches, hotel administrators and office staff find community, training, moral support, and hope. Even people who may be treated all week like machines or animals—tools for somebody else to use—here recover their dignity, their amazing worth.

Bible Study Discussion Guide

1. How did Indra prepare for her ministry? Consider both her study and her personal interactions.

2. What activities does Indra do regularly in order to expand her outreach and serve more people? To disciple people and help them understand the gospel better? To comfort people and help them sense that God is with them?

3. How does this ministry "give back" to the community?

4. What are the family challenges in this congregation?

5. What do you learn about multiethnic church networks from this chapter?

Read and discuss this text about
WOMEN WHO ARE NOBODIES:
Isaiah 54

You can't marry me." Antonia smiled. "Locals can't marry expatriates. That's the rule. Unless the local is handicapped. And you're not." She lifted one shoulder in a shrug, and smiled again.

But Adib had fallen in love.

Antonia was a nurse. One evening, when another nurse was invited to sing for an event at the Sheraton Hotel, Antonia joined the group that went along to lend moral support.

Adib was a handsome, capable civil servant employed in a government department. Now and then he enjoyed dinner at the Sheraton, and he happened to be in the hotel on the evening when Antonia's friend sang. When Antonia caught his eye, Adib nudged the elbows of mutual friends until he got himself introduced.

That is how it all began.

When Adib sent her flowers during the weeks that followed, Antonia was flattered. When he asked her out for coffee in well-lighted places, she did not feel threatened. It was a pleasant diversion in her somewhat lonely life. Filipinas love to be sociable. They love food. They love to relax. As a hard-working nurse who cleaned up after other people all day long, Antonia found it pleasant to be treated to nice things. Adib had the money to do that. No one else in Antonia's circle, either here or back home, could spend on her so lavishly. It was fun to be fussed over. And it was fun to flirt just a little, to roll eyes and giggle and maintain a sparkling repartee with this man who respected her as a professional. Having lived and worked in several countries, Adib had a cosmopolitan appreciation for other cultures. And he was smitten with Antonia.

"Marry me," he proposed.

"I am sorry," Antonia demurred. "I am a born-again Christian. You're a Muslim."

"I respect your faith. I will never ask you to give it up," he promised, and he kept sending flowers.

When Antonia's contract ended, she went home to the Philippines. But the world is not an impossible mystery for an experienced traveler. So, to Antonia's amazement, Adib arrived for a visit. What could she do? She introduced him to her family. They welcomed him with true Filipino hospitality. He gave them gifts and treated them courteously. Antonia guided him around. He was delighted to learn about the places where she had grown up. Of course she was touched by his interest.

"Marry me," he said again.

"No, I'm sorry," she answered again.

Adib reluctantly departed for home.

Eventually the time came when Antonia needed to return to the Middle East to earn money. In order to protect herself from temptation, she did not return to Adib's country but took a job in another nation. However, Adib soon showed up there.

"Please marry me," he cajoled.

Back in her room, Antonia wrestled with her conscience. "Be not unequally yoked together," she read in 2 Corinthians. Yet she began to wonder, "Lord, could this be the man who is meant to be my husband?"

She consulted her parents. They gave their blessing.

"I don't know how I fell in love with him," Antonia says now. "Somehow it just happened."

So they married.

THE MUSLIM HUSBAND

Seventeen years have passed. Now they have two sons and a lot of love still flowing between them. Antonia continues to work as a nurse. Adib has retired from government service, and is pursuing some independent initiatives.

In the beginning, Adib's family was aghast. "If she will not become a Muslim, you cannot marry her," his uncle declared.

Adib consulted the *mufti*. That religious official's ruling was more encouraging: "Yes, you can marry Antonia without converting her."

Still, the family hated her. "I'm sorry. I cannot accept her because she is not of the true faith," Adib's first cousin said.

"You are not respecting all religions," Adib retorted.

To Antonia, Adib said, "Our love is enough. Don't worry about my family."

"At first his family could not believe that a Christian and Muslim could marry and be blessed by God," Antonia says. "But they have seen that God has blessed us tremendously. They have changed their mentality. Now they greet me pleasantly." She even can chat with the uncle and the cousin without wearing a head covering or an *abaya*.

Her Christian fellowship suffered, however. "At first it was very hard. He didn't let me go to church for five years. But it was OK to pray, read the Bible, and watch Christian TV services at home."

When on the street she met friends from her former Bible study group, they would greet her, "Oh, are you a Muslim now? (*Ah, Muslim ka na?*)"

"No," she would answer. "Please pray for me."

"And maybe they did," she muses, because five years later Adib allowed her to start going to church regularly. By now she felt ashamed to go to the house church that she had attended before, so she went to the venerable mainline Protestant church. It was convenient because a member gave her a ride. Yet she didn't grow spiritually. She just went to church and returned home. There was no personal Bible study or prayer group.

One day one of her maids asked her, "Are you a Muslim?"

"No," she answered.

"Oh, maybe you would like to attend our Bible study?" the maid invited.

Here Antonia found fellowship. That group also advised her, "Go back to your original house church." So she did, and has continued there ever since.

Prayer for a child was one of her biggest requests. After giving birth to her first son, she had two miscarriages. She wrote to the 700 Club TV program and got support from Christians around the world. She and Adib also sought medical assistance. Antonia conceived and delivered a second healthy boy. "We owe him to the prayers of many," she says.

After ten years of marriage, Antonia applied for local citizenship. For a foreign Christian, such a status is not easy to obtain, but by the grace of God she became a citizen without converting.

When subordinates in the hospital learn that she is a citizen who is Christian, they sometimes treat her badly. So do superiors. She has been denied promotions. The director continually urges her to become Muslim. Colleagues dump the dirty work on her. But she closes her ears to whatever persecution comes her way and continues to treat all staff and patients equally, whether they are VIPs or prisoners, or whoever they may be.

The fruits of the Holy Spirit in her work build a platform for her words of witness. "All the Indians and all the Filipinos who are at my workplace know that Christ is Lord in my heart. They know that if I pray it will be answered by God." They come to her. "Please, sister Antonia, will you pray about my son who is having cerebral palsy?" And after God answers the prayer, Antonia tells them, "Because Christ is in my heart, because I have accepted him, I can come to him and he hears me."

MUSLIM CHILDREN

"It's very, very difficult, but God has helped me a lot," she comments. Most painful is her ache for her family. Adib and the boys came to church with her once on Father's Day after she begged—"because I need to introduce you, I need to show them that I have children."

"This is the first and the last time," Adib said. Yet on Mother's Day he joined her again.

Adib rarely goes to worship at the mosque. He doesn't like the sermons of the *mufti*. They are always striking at the religion of the Christians, he says. By contrast, on those rare occasions when he has attended church, he has been impressed by the sermons, in which the pastor advises his listeners to love and be good to others. Mosque sermons emphasize criticism of unbelievers. So it's better to stay at home and pray there, he says.

Influenced by his school, their teenage son Omar is becoming more zealous as a Muslim. "Papa, Islam says we should go to the mosque!'"

"How can we go there when they are saying bad things about other religions?" Adib asks.

So Omar too prays at home. However, for the *Id* celebrations or for funerals or marriages, father and sons do go to the mosque to participate in the prayers.

One day Omar was haranguing his mother. "Why are you saying that Jesus is the son of God? God has no son."

Adib intervened. "You need to respect what God has given to you because she is your mother. Without your mother you would not be here on earth, so you have to respect her."

Omar mellowed, and now treats her more kindly.

When her children were growing up, Antonia taught them Bible stories. She prayed openly with them at bedtime in Jesus' name. Muslims call this kind of prayer *doa*. Sometimes Adib and Antonia pray together too. She taught him. He begins, "Lord . . . ," and she concludes, "In Jesus' name."

Once in a while she shares Bible verses with Adib. He has enjoyed dipping into the book of Proverbs. "Oh Antonia, this is very nice," he will say, and will read her a verse. On occasion he has even quoted Scripture to her, such as Jeremiah 29:11. "Antonia, did you forget that God has plans for us, plans to prosper us and not to harm us, to give us a hope and a future? Did you forget that nothing is impossible with God?" A visiting Filipino pastor also has shared with Adib the story of God's complete work in Christ.

"My life now as a Christian is divided," Antonia admits. "In the Philippines I had a music ministry in the church as a member of the choir. Here, whatever opportunities come to me, whether to lead a Bible study or to teach children, whatever service I can offer, I'm grabbing."

Adib will not allow her to be a deacon or to hold a position that would require lasting commitment. An Arab wants first commitment to the family, she says. Nor can she attend church every Friday, because that is the day for the family. Adib allows her to go on alternate Fridays.

Her favorite scriptures are Psalm 1, Romans 8:28, and Jeremiah 29:11, but she especially resonates with Job. "Whenever I read about his life, I can connect with the sufferings and afflictions. But always God was there to help, to protect. . . . As for my life, it's difficult. . . . I can feel that I'm not serving God fully. . . . But I chose this. Now I have to persevere. . . . Prayer is the only weapon I have in my life, plus the word of God, and the support of church and the Bible study group. . . . My husband is a very good man. I believe 'you and your house will be saved' and I claim that someday, somehow, my family will be with Christ."

SINGLES' CHALLENGES

In the beginning, God said it was not good for man to be alone. So he created Eve. Today maids, nurses, construction laborers, office workers, and hotel personnel head for the Middle East. There they discover Adam's dilemma. It is not easy to be alone. Many of them long for a partner. What to do? Some enter into romances with other migrant workers. Some become promiscuous. Some nurture relationships with potential partners back home, then get married to those home-country partners when they travel back on their annual leave. Sometimes the new spouse can get a visa to join them in the Middle East. That is not possible for the lowest paid workers, like maids and construction workers, but may be an option for others.

If living together year-round is not an option, they will remain "holiday spouses," travelling to each other's locations for reunion trysts. A few, like Antonia, marry local people.

Cultivating healthy, happy family roles and relationships is a stormy issue roiling the currents of people flowing across the world today. How do such nomads find good spouses? Many do not. Some have learned to enjoy single life and have discovered avenues for growth and service, like Chelsea the maid and Abby the nurse, as we saw in chapters 1 and 5. If they had been able to live and work in their home country, singleness might not have been their first choice. Yet they have discovered blessings in this role. Sometimes they do feel lonely, however, not only for a husband but also for children.

The happiest singles intentionally nurture a network of friends. Many also invest in steady relationships with children, whether as "aunties" to friends' children, or through teaching children in church, or even as single mothers, natural or adoptive. Some enjoy a friendship with an older woman who serves as a mentor. Volunteer service can enrich singles' lives. So can serious hobbies, including sports and music groups. A balance of physical and mental activities is ideal. Regular prayer and praise also will lift up the spirits.

Some international churches in the Middle East sponsor singles' fellowships with serious Bible study and prayer as well as lots of food and fun. Participants may come from across the globe, from Europe, Africa, South and East Asia, Australia, North America, South America, and of course the Middle East. Here footloose and adventurous people find friends. Sometimes their faith is renewed, and some find faith for the first time.

MARRIAGE CHALLENGES

Married people struggle, too. Many are separated by thousands of miles. This opens the door to temptations. An accountant in a big firm, Suzi lives in a dorm with seventy-three other guest workers. A lot of her dormmates have husbands back home. Yet "they hang up the phone after talking with their husbands, then zoom out the door with their boyfriends." When she begs them to remember their marriage vows, they call her a spoilsport. "But marriages break up," she notes.

Pastor Indra ministers to poor Indian laborers and maids whose five-year contracts may not include a break for travel home. In such a situation, "temporary marriages" have evolved. As described in chapter 7, a migrant man approaches a woman worker and proposes an arrangement.

"Would you like to live with me for the next few years?" he says. "I'll pay your expenses, and you can send all your money home. When our time is finished, I'll return to my wife and you'll return to your husband. But while we're here, we could make a home together. Are you interested?"

Such temporary monogamy is seen as a moral improvement over promiscuity. In any case, the laborers hardly expect their spouses back home to be celibate during the long time that they are away.

How can separated spouses keep their marriages strong? In chapter 10 we will meet Lily and Artur, who were separated for ten years, with occasional reunions. Before Artur left home, they took a hard look at the pressures and temptations they would face and renewed their vows of commitment. After Artur departed, each of them got immersed in a local church where they were surrounded by activities and accountability. Of course they Skyped regularly. They even celebrated communion together over Skype. They also made air tickets and vacations a high priority, getting together as often as possible.

A couple like this will dream together and invest in common long-term projects, like a house or business or ministry. Ultimately they envision being together year-round. That is what happened to Artur and Lily. After ten years apart, she joined him in the Middle East, and for the past fifteen years they have lived and worked and ministered here together.

Charis and Ellis foster two thousand migrant believers in churches that represent a variety of countries, as described in chapter 4. Part of their ministry is marriage counseling. "Struggles are normal," they tell couples, especially newlyweds. "Every couple passes through them. The enemy attacks marriage. So we need to filter what comes into our minds, especially at times when we feel offended. As for us"—Charis and Ellis smile at each other—"our relationship is good because we work it out."

For women, Charis has more specific advice. "Watch how you dress. Or what photos you post on Facebook. We are not in the Philippines or in the US. We are in the Middle East. If we want to be respected by the people of this land, we must dress right."

Be careful in your friendships, too, she says. "Whenever we see a married person close to a single of another gender, we confront them in order to prevent trouble. Also, we advise people to stick to their own gender in discipling."

Finally, she advises, "Rather than being tempted, go home every six months. Or tell us the truth about your temptations, and we may be able to help you even to the extent of buying a ticket."

Realistically, however, most workers' contracts allow them only one short vacation a year. For others, the break comes every two years. Even those vacations may be difficult to secure. And some laborers have no break for five years. Furthermore, the workers with the fewest benefits regarding vacation time also may be too poor to telephone home regularly. And if they lack literacy or funds or permission from their employers, they may not be able to communicate by internet either.

Yet not all is bleak. In fact, the diaspora experience has strengthened some marriages. "Many families are helped because of what happens here," Charis says. For example, Ferdi came to the Lord while working in the Middle East. Before that, he used to beat his wife and his daughter. He went home a changed man. Eddy chased after women all the time. He too came to the Lord in the Gulf. "After he went home, and we happened to meet his wife in the Philippines, she started to cry right in front of us. She was so grateful to us." For many like Ferdi and Eddy, their spiritual birthplace is the Middle East. Back home, their hearts may have been so far from the Lord. Charis says, "There is a blessing in poverty if it forces you to go overseas to work, and going out in poverty you find Christ."

In Auntie Faith's Bible study group, as described in chapter 6, there is a woman who "had a terrible life before. She was doing lots of crazy things, sleeping with various men. One day she met someone who shared the gospel and brought her to the Bible study. Now she is so thankful. And there are lots of stories like this."

PARENTING CHALLENGES

Children complicate matters exponentially. As Mark Twain said, "A baby is an inestimable blessing and bother." Nowhere is this more truly the case than in migrant families.

Relatives play a crucial role in raising children in many of the countries from which the workers come. A citizen of Nigeria, Esther feels the absence of her kin keenly. Although she was born the seventh child, and her father died when she was only seven years old, Esther succeeded in graduating from college with a degree in business administration. Now she lives with her Nigerian husband in the Middle East, where he works as a medical technologist and she is an administrative assistant. Both of their children have been born here during the five years that they have worked in the Gulf.

"It was a little bit hard when Miriam was born," she says. "In Nigeria you hardly need to touch the baby for six months. There are people all around who help bathe the baby and so on. But here after one week friends disappear. Life is so busy."

Still, Esther is very positive about the church in the Gulf. "Thank God for the family of God, for the church. They remove the isolation." She and her husband attend both an international church and a local African fellowship. They need the latter, she says, because "Nigeria is communal life. The African church here provides friends that come to your home. Last Friday somebody gave birth and everybody gathered at the church for the naming ceremony. The same for my son's birthday." Still, she misses her mother. "There's nothing I can't share with her. I call her almost every day." Esther would like to bring her mother for a visit, but visas for Nigerians have been rejected.

Far different from Esther, Ginger was a single mother who left her children with their grandparents when she took a job in the Middle East, as we saw in chapter 3. This is the pattern that many parents follow. Unfortunately, even the best grandparents age. As they do, their abilities to parent will weaken. Meanwhile, children left behind may wonder about their worth. Parents try to compensate by sending money, but without adequate guidance and accountability, teens often squander it. Some get hooked on drugs. "In the Philippines we are raising a fatherless generation," Charis comments, and advises bluntly, "If you're financially stable and you have children there, go home."

Esther's children are lucky enough to grow up in the bosom of their nuclear family in the Middle East. Schooling can be a challenge, however. The local schools operate in Arabic, and usually are not open to foreign laborers' children. Furthermore, citizenship will not be available to the children here. When they become adults, they will be required to return to their parents' country. That will mean erasing a big part of their identity. Where is home? They may feel like aliens everywhere they try to settle.

Sometimes the problems are more elementary. One parent asks, "What can we do for family fun? Where can we take our kids during the holidays? We go to the desert and take photos with camels. But there is not the natural or cultural variety that we would have back home. The kids ask, 'Why can't we live a normal life? Ride bikes? Have a backyard?'" This family doesn't allow their eighth-grade daughter to ride a bike, because there have been many rapes. The girl misses it. The children do play musical instruments, sing together, and raise small pets, and they have travelled as a family on a ministry trip across Europe.

CHILDLESS CHALLENGES

Children don't always arrive, however, even when a couple longs for them. Linda waited for twelve years before the first of her two children was born. Josie prayed a long time for a baby, and then lost him five days after birth. Xena never has been able to bear a child.

The Gulf has shaped Xena deeply. It is where she grew spiritually, where her husband came to faith, and where they met and married. Together they have taken classes in Christian leadership. Now they lead an extension church. However, they have no children.

"You have spiritual children," people console them. But they ache for a baby that they can hug in their arms 24/7. Now, through a route that nobody would have predicted, God is giving them a baby. Back home in the Philippines, a pregnant teenager gave birth prematurely. Xena's mother heard about the baby and asked for it. Through a friend of a friend, the infant was passed into her care. Today that baby is seven months old, healthy and blossoming. Xena and her husband are going home soon to claim their child and bring her back to brighten their future in the Arabian Gulf.

Unquestionably, laboring in another country strains families. Elderly parents, adult brothers and sisters, and other kin miss the overseas worker, sometimes acutely. In this area there are many gaping wounds that will not diminish in the foreseeable future. Missiologists and mission administrators therefore ought to direct compassionate research to focus on these diaspora relational realities. These families' and singles' challenges deserve higher priority attention from brothers and sisters in the global church.

But some families flourish . . .

WHEN A FAMILY FLOURISHES

The apostles shimmered in gold, rose, and green on painted walls. Wrapped in a blue robe, beautiful mother Mary gazed down from the heights. Incense wafted upward. Water dampened fingertips and foreheads. Bells reverberated. Choir voices harmonized ancient liturgies, rising up in thirds and fourths and fifths. That is how God came to Claudia as a child. Rarely was the Bible read in her home. Only at Christmas and Easter would her parents take the sacred Scriptures in their hands. Then the words of the old story would resonate humbly but confidently through her father's and mother's voices.

Yes, strange things did happen from time to time in the world of Philippine Catholicism, such as the penitents who lashed their bloodied backs in processions at Easter, and even volunteered to be nailed to crosses in order to fulfill some vow. Or the Black Nazarene in the big shabby cathedral in Quiapo in Manila, and the magical use of his image by poor and desperate people. Or the circle hired to sing the *Pasyon,* the epic of the passion of Christ, giving voice to the gorgeous classic Tagalog but slurring the words as they imbibed their pay in rice wine.

Far from all that, Claudia spent her days dressed in a white blouse, blue skirt, blue tie, and shined shoes. She and her friends giggled, nudged, and bounced through the halls, then quieted with respect when the teaching nun entered the classroom, dignified as a ship sailing on a calm sea even though she smelled like chalk. Over in the parish church, Father Ortega bridged between the mysteries of the universe and the ordinary cycle of life. Catholicism gave meaning and significance to Claudia's world, emphasizing morality, strong marriages, helpful neighbors, honest businesses, and care for the needy.

With the inexorable passing of the seasons, the fidgeting girls grew into svelte young ladies and became wives and mothers. Claudia fell in love with a boy named Elmer. They were well suited. Both came from strong, stable, well-connected families. Like Claudia, Elmer had attended private Catholic schools in Manila. Both of them valued Christian heritage and tradition. Joyfully they married, and poured their energies into building a happy family.

Within ten years they were juggling five children, without enough money to cover all the bills.

"When will I quit buying diapers?" Elmer muttered. One by one the children were enrolled in private schools. That was the kind of education that Claudia and Elmer had enjoyed. They wanted nothing less for their children. But the tuition expenses mounted.

Both Elmer's and Claudia's parents slipped them extra money. "How much is the tuition this year?" Claudia's mother-in-law would ask when she phoned. "Ah, so much. Well, I'll just send you a check to cover your electric bill."

That was loving, but also humiliating. With their fine educations and excellent work habits, Claudia and Elmer thought they should be able to stand on their own. So Elmer took a job overseas. He helped administer a construction project on an island in the Indian Ocean. The company was Filipino, working on a classified joint US-British project.

When that job finished, Elmer returned home. For a couple of years he served on a congressman's team. However, when the political picture changed, Elmer was scrambling for work once more.

"After that, it was hand to mouth," Claudia remembers.

Meanwhile, half a world away, Saddam Hussein's Iraqi forces invaded Kuwait. The US embassy was bombed. Before long, Iraqi forces were pushed back. Kuwait began tackling the rubble of war. It was time to rebuild the US embassy. Elmer had experience supervising construction teams and working with American officials. He landed a job here. Later, because of his exemplary work, he was invited to stay on at the embassy, moving into the financial department.

"Will I have the opportunity to bring my family here?" he asked.

"Yes," he was assured. So Claudia and all five children, ages five to sixteen, arrived to settle into a new home in the Middle East. Since the children needed English-language schools and there were no Filipino schools yet, they enrolled in local Indian schools.

Claudia also went looking for a Protestant church.

While Elmer had been working overseas, Claudia had embarked on a new spiritual journey. Prior to his departure, she had been employed in a bank. When he left, she resigned from her job in order to provide the parenting that the children would need. Because she participated actively in her children's school activities, Claudia was elected to the school board. There she met Cora, who was a born-again Christian.

One day Claudia saw that Cora was in the throes of organizing an activity for her church. Because Claudia was lonely, she was looking for opportunities to be useful. "Cora, what can I do to help you? What is this activity that seems so overwhelming?" she asked.

"The PCEC is organizing a 'March for Jesus,'" Cora told her. For the first time Claudia heard about the Philippine Council of Evangelical Churches. "We're having a hard time finding a venue that is big enough for the event," Cora explained.

Claudia knew the city officials. Their children had been her classmates. "I'll ask the mayor. Let's go to his house," she said.

"No problem," said the mayor after they explained the issue. "You can march, and you can build a stage in front of Quezon City Hall." Quezon City is the capital of the Philippines.

"What else can I do?" Claudia asked Cora.

"Bishop Efraim is going to be installed at Greenhills Christian Fellowship. We need ushers. Would you like to help out?" This was one of the most esteemed Protestant churches in the country.

"I would enjoy it. But what will I say if they ask what church I'm from? Can I tell them I'm from Our Lady of the Miraculous Medal?" Claudia wondered.

"Just say you work for PCEC."

Over the next few months, Claudia did a lot of volunteer work for PCEC. She enjoyed the people. The projects were worthwhile. In the worship services, she sensed the presence of God. Unknown to her, other volunteers and staff prayed for her. But no one intruded with questions.

After the ordination of Bishop Efraim, Claudia began attending Greenhills Christian Fellowship regularly. "Pastor Ef was so gentle in sharing. I heard the word of God. That's where my heart opened."

Another pastor, Luis Pantoja, would recite the poem titled "Invictus" by William Ernest Henley. Claudia identified with that, because she had studied it in school:

> Out of the night that covers me,
> Black as the Pit from pole to pole,
> I thank whatever gods may be
> For my unconquerable soul.
>
> . . . .
>
> It matters not how strait the gate,
> How charged with punishments the scroll,
> I am the master of my fate,
> I am the captain of my soul.

The day came when Claudia found herself asking, "Pastor Ef, may I have a Bible?" She had always said, "I don't want to study theology or religion. From elementary school, I've studied it. I've had enough study." Yet now she found herself reading, as well as fellowshipping and worshiping.

One Sunday in November the pastor issued an invitation to those in the congregation. "Stand up if you want to receive Jesus in your heart."

Claudia stood up. "It was embarrassing. My classmates were there," she remembers. But she could not stay seated.

So when Claudia landed in the Middle East, she went searching for a church. That made Elmer uneasy. Of course he knew about her spiritual progression. He had even had passing contact with Bishop Ef when that pastor had visited the Gulf.

When Claudia had heard that the bishop was going to travel to that region, she had made a request. "Can I send a letter to my husband with you?"

"Of course, Claudia," the bishop had replied.

Upon their arrival in the Gulf, Bishop Ef's assistant had contacted Elmer. "Come to this church to get your wife's letter."

Elmer came, but he remained on a bench outside. "Ever since we were small, we were taught that if you go inside a Protestant church it is a sin," Claudia explains. "And every religious book that we read had to have the imprimatur of the church."

"Go inside!" urged Elmer's friend. "You didn't make an appointment with pastor Ef, you made an appointment with the Lord." Eventually Elmer did meet pastor Ef and get his letter. But he did not enter the church.

And now his family wanted to attend a Protestant church!

"Honey, we might commit mortal sin. Let's go to the Catholic church first, and then to the Protestant," Elmer negotiated.

Claudia agreed. Meanwhile, she discovered a women's group called Wellsprings, and found fellowship there.

But soon the children were protesting. "Papa, let's not go to the other church anymore."

"Why?"

"Because we're not doing anything there. Just sitting, standing, kneeling. But we learn a lot in the Protestant church."

The first Protestant church they tried was Pentecostal. During the service, there was prophesying. This proved to be too strange for Elmer and Claudia. So they tried another church. Here the congregation sang hymns. Claudia recognized some of them. They both liked *Great Is Thy Faithfulness*. Elmer began to learn some of the songs.

After one service, the worship leader went up to Elmer. "The Lord told me that you play an instrument," he said.

"Uh . . . yes."

"What instrument?"

"Guitar."

"Would you like to come to practice with our music team?"

"OK."

Claudia joined the music team too. Eventually their older son would manage the sound system. Hearing the Word during two services every Sunday as they served on the music team, they all grew spiritually. Over time they have helped to develop the Lighthouse Church, which shines as a bright beacon in the Middle East.

Just as she spent her days in active service when she lived in the Philippines, Claudia is not idle in the Gulf. Besides helping her husband, her five children, and her church, Claudia teaches kindergarten at Lighthouse Academy. She continues to fellowship with the women's group, Wellsprings. She is part of a team that visits runaway maids who have taken sanctuary in the embassy. She also helps disciple working maids. "Many maids have grown in the Lord," she says.

In her daily life, Claudia is a good neighbor. The family lives not in a ghetto or gated community for foreigners but in a local neighborhood. "When neighbors visit, we share our story." She has given the JESUS film to local people, and also to an Egyptian. She always has Arabic Bibles and audiotapes at hand.

Some Filipinas are married to local men. Claudia gets together with them naturally because of the children. She plays English-language kids' "praise CDs" when the families visit, and loans them out. Soon the kids memorize the verses of the songs and sing them on their own. When they hear the name of a Bible character they say, "I know that," especially if the character is also in the Quran, like Noah. Jesus is known to the children as a healer and miracle-worker.

Claudia and Elmer have shared the gospel with three of these mixed families. Now the wives and children come to church with their husbands' blessings. Some of the women wear head coverings to the services. Some now worship Jesus as Lord. "Almost a whole family has come to saving grace," Claudia confides.

One neighbor who is a policeman went to church with them. They had invited him to bring the police team to see the school. He sat at the back of the church during the service. Afterwards he commented, "You know, you worship like us. We lift our hands. And we pray to God. We don't pray to the saints. Directly to God. So do you."

In the Arabian Gulf, some migrants are single and others are married, some couples are separated in space and others are together, some are parents and others are childless. All have stresses, but at least they can reach out to brothers and sisters in the faith because "God sets the solitary in families" (Ps 68:6).

Bible Study Discussion Guide

1. Singleness, marriage, child-raising, and childlessness
   all present challenges. Which of these stories and issues
   touched you the most? Have you struggled with any of
   these areas yourself?

2. How will you pray differently for these women after
   reading about these issues?

3. What surprised you in the story of marriage to a Muslim?

4. Claudia always has Arabic Bibles and videos on hand to
   share with neighbors and friends. How could a mission
   you support provide these resources for migrant workers in
   the Gulf?

Read and discuss these texts about
THE FAMILY:
Psalm 127, Psalm 128, and Psalm 133

CHAPTER NINE

The Faiths

While working in one of the most restrictive countries in the world, Josie came to faith in Jesus.

Her family roots were in a little island near Boracay. This is a spectacular, world-famous diving resort. But Josie's island was poor. Her family had lived in Manila when she was small. However, when her dad lost his job, the family moved back to the countryside. Josie was in her second year of high school at that time. She could picture her future slipping away. There was no electricity in their rural home. The nearest neighbor was distant. Josie determined that she would not get stuck there. She would get out. And she did. After studying hard, she graduated as a nurse and took a job in Manila.

A few years later she travelled to the Middle East in order to make even more money.

In the country where Josie was employed, the society was strict. She worked in an oncology ward and lived in a dorm with one hundred nurses. Since the dorm and the hospital were connected, they ate, slept, and worked without ever leaving the complex. Twelve-hour shifts were the norm. The gates were kept locked, and the nurses were not allowed to go out by themselves. Company busses were provided for shopping trips. IDs stayed behind in the dorm. Married nurses had to carry their marriage certificates with them if they wanted to walk down the street with their husbands.

Josie had signed up to room with friends, but when she discovered that the woman across the hall was alone, she could not help asking, "Would you like me to be your roommate to keep you company?" Filipinos feel sorry for people who are all by themselves.

"Yes, please. I'd like that very much," answered the women, whose name was Aurora.

The roommates discovered that they both liked to read. In their free time they would sit comfortably side by side, each immersed in her own book. Often Aurora would read the Bible. That surprised Josie.

"Wow, I didn't think we were allowed to bring Bibles in!" she said.

"We're not, but I had contacts here and someone gave me one."

Out of the corner of her eye, Josie watched Aurora. She saw Christianity lived out in her roommate's daily habits. Now and then they talked about what Aurora was reading in the Bible. At Thanksgiving, Aurora invited Josie to a worship service. This was secret, because in this country no Christian worship services are permitted. At this event, the speaker invited people to make a commitment to follow Jesus as Lord. Josie was ready. Her weeks with Aurora had prepared her, and she responded to the invitation. "I had an open heart. They did not have a hard time sharing Christ with me," she says.

Perhaps her brother had prepared her too. He had committed his life to Christ while they were in high school, and he had prayed for Josie. In other respects, however, he was a poor witness. When he was supposed to be doing household chores, he would lie on the couch and read the Bible. "One day you'll go crazy reading the Bible," she told him. On weekends, when he was supposed to be fetching water and chopping wood, he would go to the city to attend fellowship meetings. "Don't give him money," Josie complained to her father.

"But maybe I am the answer to my brother's prayers," she says now. "And maybe that's why I came here. Maybe the Lord said, 'I can deal with you better if you are in this hard place.'"

At any rate, it was here that Josie began to grow as a disciple of Jesus.

Once when a group of five nurses were meeting and singing together, someone in the dorm reported them to the administration. They were summoned to appear before the director of the nursing program. She was British.

"Are you engaging in Christian worship?" she asked them.

"Yes," they answered honestly, and they told her about their activities. "But here in the dorm we stay in one room when we worship, and we don't disturb anybody."

"Well, if British nurses are caught doing this kind of thing, our embassy will help. But your embassy is not in a position to do much. So my advice to you is to stop this Christian worship, or else go home. It's for your own good," she counselled them.

At that point the Christians quit using the guitar and worshipped even more discreetly. Yet some of the women's contracts were not renewed. They had exhibited "failure to comply with the customs of the country." With tears flowing down her face, Josie waved goodbye when her friends boarded the airport bus. *What will I do now that I'm alone, Lord?* she prayed. Her departing friends had mentored and discipled her. They had become like family.

Now, years later, she comments, "If God takes something or somebody from your life, he will replace it. The Bible study began again, and this time I was the one leading it."

Josie got materials from an underground church. After dinner she would ask friends, "Are you available? Come to my room and we'll study."

The numbers increased. They started using the guitar again, and even Josie learned to play it "in a limited way—but not praise songs because they're too fast." The group chose songs that she could handle until God brought along someone who could play better. Then Josie concentrated on the Word. Sometimes they were just a group of three, but they claimed the promise that where two or three are gathered together in the name of Jesus, God is there (Matt 18:20).

In the pediatric ward, the head nurse was a Filipina named Alva. Some of the Bible study members worked under her. Josie got to know her too. Although Alva had converted to Islam, she enjoyed talking with Josie and her friends. Because she was a few years older, they viewed her almost as a mother figure. Visits to her apartment were special.

What a shock it was to discover that Alva was spying on members of the Bible study and reporting on them to the authorities. "We felt so betrayed."

That was not the end of the story, however. Alva was discovered to be pregnant. From her supervisory position she was demoted to staff nurse, which is hard work for a pregnant woman.

"God is our vindicator. We don't have to repay evil for evil. God will bless those who bless us and curse those who curse us," Josie says.

Looking back over her six years in this restrictive country, Josie says, "Now I see the wonderful plan of God for me." Not only did she come to faith in this surprising place. She also grew to maturity. "When I was left behind, the Lord said, 'You can stand alone. I will be with you.'" It was here that she developed leadership skills. Since then, those skills have served her well in other Gulf countries.

ISLAM AND CHRISTIANITY

Why wasn't Josie allowed to worship freely?

As we saw in chapter 5 in the stories of Abby and Emma, Muslims and Christians share many doctrines and ethical principles. Both believe in a God who is all-powerful and holy, the creator of the cosmos, the sustainer of all the systems of the universe, and the one who will culminate history in his own time. Both faiths teach that God cares enough to communicate with people through the amazing designs of nature, through prophets, and through Scriptures. Both affirm that humans are called to worship God and live ethically according to God's laws, taking care of God's earth. Muslims consciously classify themselves with Christians and Jews as a group that is distinct from Buddhists, Hindus, Taoists, Shintoists, or other religionists. This is because the three "Abrahamic religions" possess Scriptures that have come from God, according to Muslims.

The crucial difference regards the person and work of Jesus. While Muslims honor Jesus as a great prophet, they consider it blasphemy to say that he is God. Also, most Muslims believe Jesus did not die on the cross. When tumult led to a crucifixion,

God snatched Jesus away so that he would not suffer and be shamed. Someone else died in his place.

This is not a trivial difference. It is the pivot of the Christian faith. Christians believe that the greatness of God is shown not just in creating the universe, keeping it together, and bringing it to a culmination. Not just in demonstrating wisdom and power and righteousness. Not just in pouring mercy on us by placing us in a wonderfully designed world, giving us families and communities, and sending us scriptures to guide us. God's greatness is most powerfully revealed in his grace, which is rolled out in Jesus' life, death, resurrection, and reign. To paraphrase T. S. Eliot, the timeless one entered time, and redeemed it from insignificance. The Creator entered death and broke its power on the cosmic level. This is the true greatness of God. That is the testimony of Jesus' people.

Clearly this difference between Christianity and Islam goes deep. Yet why should it limit Josie's worship in a Muslim-majority country?

The stories of two men may help us understand a little more. First, the Prophet Muhammad. When he was born, approximately five hundred years after Jesus' time, Arabia was a place of deserts and oases and small coastal cities. Trade rippled across the land and the sea. Most people worshipped spirits, but Jews and nominal Christians were tied into the trading networks too. The *kaaba*, which is the physical center of Muslim worship in Mecca today, at that time housed 360 gods. It was a destination for religious pilgrims who came to worship the gods. There was also a long tradition of *hanifs*, people who sought to worship God with more purity and focus and simplicity.

Muhammad was a merchant who traveled throughout the region. When he was home, he occasionally retreated into a cave for spiritual meditation. There God's angel visited him, he said. Out of the angel's revelations developed the Quran, which Muslims consider the authoritative scripture. Among its teachings, the Quran includes stories of men and women whose lives also are described in the Bible, such as Adam, Abraham, Mary, and Jesus. Muhammad's trading undoubtedly brought him into contact with Jews and Christians. Unfortunately, neither the Old nor New Testament had been translated into Arabic at that time.

Muhammad's great contribution to the Arab people, and eventually to others, was his emphasis on one God. Though surrounded by idolaters, he insisted on one God, high and holy. Soon this unity in the heavens became a model for unity on earth and inclined Arab tribes to connect beyond their clans, even though fighting continued. (Yes, Jews proclaimed one God. But Jews had not fulfilled their call to be light to the nations. Muslims bypassed them, soon spreading monotheism from Spain to Southeast Asia.)

Ethics were part of Muhammad's teaching, including charity for the poor and safeguards for women. (Non-Muslim critics may complain that Muhammad financed his movement by leading raids on camel caravans, and that he sometimes married dubiously, including a child bride. But we will focus here on his positive contributions.)

Those who accepted Muhammad's monotheism became the *ummah*, the community of believers. For Muslims this community is central. Reorienting your life toward the one God and learning to live ethically cannot be done in isolation.

Godly habits require reinforcement. Therefore Muslim religion is public. Daily corporate prayers; an annual month-long fast (with feasting at night); recitation of the creed in unison in the mosque on Fridays (primarily for men); a once-in-a-lifetime pilgrimage to the holy city of Mecca if you are healthy and wealthy enough; religious feasts and celebrations; a religious tax to help the poor; and the conviction that church and state should not be separate, that law should be based on theology—all these make faith a social experience. Believers are formed and shaped in righteous patterns together.

But how does Muhammad's story relate to the limitations that Josie experienced?

The word *islam* means "submission" to God. Surely the best community is one where everybody submits to God, Muslims say. Surely this is the healthiest place for human beings to live. It is here that morality and ethics and social well-being will blossom. And if that is so, how can migrants' introducing other religions be an improvement? They can only divide and weaken and pollute the godly society. So it is better to keep other faiths out of the country altogether.

Another man took this further. His name was Ibn Abdul Wahhab.

As Islam spread in the centuries after Muhammad, it absorbed ideas from Greek philosophy and Hindu and Persian mysticism. Elements foreign to Islam crept in. These included shrines, the intercession of saints, reverence for Muhammad as eternal and central in the cosmos, pilgrimages to local power centers, and mystic ritual worship services. The Prophet Muhammad's emphasis on one God was diluted.

Ibn Abdul Wahhab was the man who cried, "Stop! This is perversion of the faith!"

Although he was born in Arabia in 1705, Wahhab studied in Persia and no doubt observed departures from orthodoxy there. After he returned home, Wahhab convinced the ancestor of the current Saudi royal family to support religious reform. When Arabia became Saudi Arabia in the 1930s, the Saudis took over politics and Wahhabis took over religious affairs. This partnership continues today. That is why the Islam in this region is among the strictest in the world. Because they have seen syncretism in their own Muslim history, Wahhabis are firm fundamentalists.

Ironically, this was the milieu where Josie came to know Jesus as Lord.

CALLED TO WITNESS

Although Christian worship is not allowed where Josie lived, it is permitted in many other Muslim countries. It is allowed in restricted areas for people who were not born into Muslim families. Such non-Muslims have not turned away from submission to God, because they never practiced it, Muslims say. These non-Muslims always were unbelievers. In most Gulf countries, there is at least one limited location where such Christians can worship.

For a person from a Muslim family, however, conversion usually is forbidden. In some cases, converts are attacked with violence or with capital punishment decreed through the courts. In milder cases, converts are expelled from their families and jobs. In still other cases, they are permitted to continue in their customary roles, but their friends and kin will try to persuade them to return to the true faith.

Nevertheless, just as Muslims are mandated to witness, so too Christians are called to witness, even to those born into Muslim families. The mercy of God is good news for everyone. It cannot be hoarded secretly. It must be offered freely.

There are many bases for witness in the common core that Muslims and Christians share. Take the story of Abraham. He had a son who was his joy. One day God said to Abraham, "I want you to show your loyalty to me. I want you to sacrifice your son."

In the religions of that day, people did offer their children as sacrifices to their gods. So Abraham prepared to kill his son.

Then God said, "That's enough! I see your heart. I see your obedience. I myself will provide an animal for the sacrifice."

God did provide an animal, and Abraham offered that instead.

Every year since then, Muslims all over the world celebrate the *Id al-Adha* feast to mark this wonderful event: Abraham's son did not have to die, because God provided a sacrifice.

Both Muslim and Christian Scriptures record this story. It points forward to the day when God would provide a sacrifice by becoming the sacrifice, the day when Jesus as the "lamb of God" would die in our place. Yet death could not hold Jesus. He exploded right through death into supernatural life, because God truly is great.

In spite of the fact that conversion out of Islam often is banned, thousands of Muslims around the world are coming to worship Jesus. Some insist that it is not necessary to leave Islam in order to follow Jesus as Lord. To be Muslim is more cultural than religious, they say. To be Muslim means submitting to God, and what could be truer submission than worshipping Jesus? These groups are known as "insider movements." Some members may continue to worship at the mosque and pray the traditional Muslim prayers. Yet they consider the Bible authoritative and testify to being born again and filled with the Holy Spirit.

Will they learn enough Bible and doctrine if they remain Muslims? Will they experience the deep community of Jesus' people? Will they be baptized and take communion? Will their children know how to lead fellowships of Jesus' followers in the next generation? These challenges lie ahead. Meanwhile, the Holy Spirit is blowing widely through the Muslim world.

Sadly, not many Gulf citizens have been caught up in this fresh wind yet.

Isaiah 60 reveals a grand procession of people from many countries who bring offerings to God. Kedar and Nebaioth, the first two sons of Ishmael, ride in that procession. They glide forward joyfully on their camels, "ships of the desert." Similarly, Revelation 5–7 shows people from all kingdoms and tribes and peoples and nations worshipping the Lamb around the throne at the end of time. Qataris, Kuwaitis, Omanis, Emiratis, Saudis, and Yemenis will be there.

To that end, we must "always be ready to give an answer for the hope that is in [us], but do it with humility and respect" (1 Pet 3:15).

WHAT HAPPENED TO JOSIE

Lord, I want to go somewhere else, Josie prayed. After six years she was ready for a new environment. Relatives back home depended on her. Nursing overseas was the only way for her to earn a significant income. Josie applied to go to the UK and US and passed the exams. Yet she felt called to return to the Gulf.

This time she chose to work in a country where there was more freedom for worship.

"And God did not abandon me," she says. "He gave me a Christian flat mate, although I did not ask for this. We came at the same time seven years ago, and have stuck together. We get along well."

"Something new" came in a different form. On a visit back to the Philippines, Josie got married. Her husband, Armando, also is a nurse. They were classmates in nursing school. Josie's brother was the one who led Armando to the Lord. Upon their marriage, Armando applied for work in the Gulf. However, his application was rejected because he was too old. The cut-off age is thirty-five. So Armando visits her regularly in the Gulf on a visitor's visa, and she stays with him on her vacations in the Philippines.

"Maybe God has another plan for us," Josie says. Maybe it will be Canada. She and Armando have applied to go there together.

Four years ago Josie and Armando got pregnant. She was thirty-three and wanted children so much. When she found out the good news, she was so happy that she was jumping, hugging everybody, hardly knowing how she managed to come down or go up the stairs because she was so filled with joy.

As she lay down for her first ultrasound, excitement and hope bubbled through her. She peered at the squiggling image and tried to discern her baby's shape. "Ooh—the legs. See the arms waving. And that little face!" It was awesome.

But the doctor cleared his throat and looked away. "I'm sorry," he told her. "Your baby is not normal. He has hydrocephalus. I know this is a huge disappointment, but we're going to have to evacuate him."

Josie could not even stand up to get off the ultrasound table because she was crying so hard. Eventually, when she could walk, she telephoned Armando.

"Stop crying," he comforted her. "I'm coming as soon as I can get a flight, and we'll talk about it then. Go home for now."

At home she wrestled with God. *Lord, I have prayed for this baby, and you have answered my prayer. Why are you taking it away from us?*

In time she was able to leave it in the Lord's hands. Her husband arrived, and after many visits to the clinic they decided to go ahead with the pregnancy "so we can at least see the baby."

"Why do you have to go on and suffer?" her doctor asked. "It will die two hours after birth."

"But we had five precious days with the baby," Josie testifies. "And I told the Lord, *This will not alter my confidence in your promise that you have a wonderful plan for me. . . . I have been knocking on the windows of heaven for you to bring me and my husband together, and for you to bring us children. I know you're working behind the scenes. I'm just waiting here.*"

While she anticipates moving to Canada, Josie shares her faith with those who ask. One day she met Lila, a nurse's aide who was waiting for a mentally disabled patient to get out of surgery. Lila was happy to encounter another Filipina.

"Ask me if you need any help. I'm not too busy today," Josie told Lila. Then, since she had free time, she pulled a book of Christian discipleship out of her pocket and began to study it.

"What's that?" Lila asked.

Josie explained the gospel, reading from various pages. When she got up to leave, Lila jumped up and said, "Sister Josie, I just want to copy that prayer that you read."

The next day Josie brought Lila a Bible and another booklet. During those two days, as they spent time together and continued their talks guided by the teaching in the book, Lila opened her heart to Jesus as Lord, and prayed and invited him into her life.

Since then Lila has returned to the Philippines. However, she continues to phone Josie and interact with her on Facebook. She has a strong debt of gratitude to Josie.

A NEW CREATION

One of Josie's favorite verses is 2 Corinthians 5:17: "If anyone is in Christ, there is a new creation." This is true, she says. "I'm not where I should be, but I have come far from where I was." Arriving in a country where she was not allowed to worship freely, much less to convert to Jesus as Lord, Josie nevertheless has experienced a transformation that is real. For example, she says, "It used to be that if people hurt me, I would just get quiet. But now I try to see Jesus in them. He died not just for me, but also for them. Then it's easy to love, when I see Jesus in them."

Prayer is a focus for her these days, "because I know that when we pray something is happening in the spiritual reality even though we cannot see it. The enemy wants to stop us from talking with God. Time will pass by. Sometimes I want to memorize verses, and then the enemy will distract me. So I talk to the Lord. I say, *Lord, I want to focus on you.*"

Josie now has spent thirteen years in the Middle East. And every morning, as she watches the sun rise over the Arabian Gulf, she opens her computer to Christian worship music and teaching.

The praises of Jesus resound because Josie is there.

Bible Study Discussion Guide

1. God is at work even in places where we cannot send missionaries. What will keep us motivated to pray for these "hidden" Christians?

2. Who is God, according to Muslims? Thank God that he is the powerful, wise creator of this whole universe.

3. Who is Jesus, according to Muslims? Thank God that he is our Savior, the one who comes close and even sacrifices his life in order to give us new life.

4. If a Muslim told you, "We also honor Jesus," what would you say?

5. If witness to Muslims is forbidden, should Christians witness?

6. "The praises of Jesus resound because Josie is there." Can people in your workplace say that about you?

Read and discuss this text about
JESUS:
Colossians 1:13–22

T hey took him on a Sunday evening. Later that night they returned and ransacked our whole place." Lily made big sweeping cartwheels with her arms. "'Where is the money?' they kept demanding."

Lily was telling me about her husband's arrest. For the two weeks following that Sunday night invasion of her home, she would not have any idea where Artur was. She would hear nothing at all. For the next forty days she would not be allowed to see him. Then they would have one hour together.

Lily and Artur have been married for twenty-seven years. Fifteen of those have been in the Arabian Gulf. They have raised their children here. Now those children have returned to the Philippines as young adults. Meanwhile, Lily and Artur continue on in the Middle East. Besides working at their day jobs, they co-pastor a church with a multiethnic English-language service as well as Filipino-language services. Filipinos, Pakistanis, Indians, Kenyans, and Nigerians all worship and fellowship together in this church.

"The first week after my husband was taken, nobody went to church. All the people stayed home and prayed. Except that one of them always stayed with me, so that nobody would be able to snatch me without anyone knowing," Lily says. "What I learned was to fully trust the Lord. Because in the beginning I was down. I was afraid."

She started to fast, and remained in a partial fast for the next two months. Isaiah 49:23–25 became precious. Verse 25 says, "Even the captives of the mighty shall be taken away, and the prey of the terrible shall be delivered: for I will contend with him who contends with you, and I will save your children." The verse also says that those who wait for the Lord will not be ashamed. Not being shamed is a key Filipino value. Lily claimed this promise.

Through it all, she had to keep on working. Like most Christian ministers in the Gulf, Lily makes her living in a regular job. She is the secretary to the senior manager of a department. Her boss is an Arab Muslim. The first week after her husband was taken, she told her boss about the situation, and asked for one day's leave so she could stay home and pray and seek God's face.

"Take three days," he said kindly.

But Lily had no family around her to help her cope. She could not even tell her children, because she suspected that the phone was tapped. Finally, with the help of a friend, she called them on a secure phone. They were shocked.

During that period, one of Artur's brothers also telephoned, expecting a friendly chat. She couldn't tell him why Artur couldn't come to the phone. She had to make up excuses about when he would call back.

She did ask the children early on for money "for a sick brother," promising to pay them back later.

Money was tight because Artur's salary was gone. Now it was up to Lily to cover all the expenses. She was the one who had to bring in income.

She was also the one who had to preach.

People kept asking, "What is the message from the Lord?"

Lily said to herself, "Why should *I* be the one who has to encourage *them*? Don't *I* need encouragement?"

Then she understood the Apostle Paul better. Even from his prison cell, he had to encourage others. She realized, "I am the one who has to preach. The Lord spoke to my mind, 'Lily, just do it. Stand up there for me. Preach the Word. No matter how you feel, set it all aside. Just preach the Word.'"

She also continued reaching out to the needy, especially to women seeking refuge in embassies and women in prison. Local churches take turns visiting these detained women every Friday, providing somebody for the detainees to talk to as well as normal things like soap or shampoo or sanitary napkins. Some of these unfortunate women do not even have a change of clothes. Recently, during the holiday for the Muslim *Id* festival, the church sponsored a women's conference, and part of the proceeds was donated to help the women in detention.

Desperate people can show up anywhere. One day a frightened-looking woman stopped Lily on the street. "Excuse me, ma'am. Do you have any money? I'm so sorry to bother you, but I can't pay my taxi fare."

Lily gave the money. Then she noticed that the woman was moving as if she was in pain. "Are you hurt?" Lily asked.

"My employer poured boiling water over my body and my legs. So I had to run away," the woman groaned.

Lily whipped out her cell phone and called a friend who was a nurse. Together they took the woman to a hospital where ointment was smoothed onto her legs. Then they took her to the police, showed them the injuries, and requested them to summon her employer.

The burned woman just wanted to go back to the Philippines. She had children waiting for her there. She had only been in the Gulf for one month.

"Look!" the policeman thundered at the employer when that man showed up. "See what your wife has done. She poured boiling water over this maid's legs. Disgraceful! You had better settle up at once. Give the woman a ticket home. Otherwise we will be forced to bring in your wife for interrogation."

Lily and the nurse stood with this injured woman and served as her advocates so the police could not ignore her. Neither could the employer. Then and there, he bought her a ticket back to the Philippines. For several more hours Lily stayed in the police station with the woman until someone brought her possessions. This was a safety measure so the woman would not have to re-enter her employer's house in order to recover her belongings.

Sometimes needy women are not abused. They are just lonely. "Women come to the Lord readily here," Lily says. "Just yesterday a Pakistani girl invited an Indian girl to the church service, and she accepted the Lord." Lily had preached on the fear of the Lord versus the fear of man, a topic on which she is well qualified to speak. Afterwards she counseled and prayed with the girl.

So life went on. Lily had not been home when her husband was taken, so she didn't see him or talk to him when he went. She wasn't able to say goodbye. After that, when she tried to find out where he was, she was completely blocked. For two weeks she had no idea what was happening to Artur or where he was being kept. She could only imagine. Then she was asked to bring a change of clothes to a certain prison. When she did, the prison returned his dirty clothes.

"I was so happy, because now I knew where he was," she remembers. "After that, I exchanged clothes with the prison weekly. That was our only communication. I never saw him. Once the prison called me for his diabetes medicine. Another time they requested rubber shoes."

At last, after forty days, she was permitted to see him for one hour. He looked terrible, but she had determined beforehand that she would not cry. And she didn't.

Meanwhile, Artur had been praying. What else was there to do? He had lots of time, so he used it to talk with the Lord, and he sensed God telling him things. He learned from God directly in the jail. Occasionally he was able to help other prisoners too. One day, for example, he sat down beside an Iranian.

"I'm worried for my family. I've been here forty days," the Iranian confided.

"I'll pray for you," Artur said.

As he prayed for the Iranian, he got the strong sense that the man was going to be freed. Artur told him about this. "God told me you'll be released."

Sure enough, the next day the Iranian was let out of the prison.

But what about Artur?

Legal protection for foreign migrant workers in these countries is not well established. There is hardly a bill of rights or list of defense attorneys that one can access. Once a person falls afoul of the powers, he or she is not freed very easily. Sometimes it feels like you are swirling down a black hole. You are tempted to abandon hope.

A WOMAN IN PRISON

Over in the women's section of the jail was a girl named Yanu. Coming from Nepal, Yanu had been working as a maid. Her job evaporated when her employer accused her of inviting a boy into her flat.

"No way," said the accused boy. "I was never there."

But Yanu admitted that it was true.

"Some other boy, then," said the employer. The boy was set free, and the employer filed a case against Yanu.

She turned herself in to the police. "I am ready to be deported," she said.

Instead she was detained in prison for six months.

After that, she expected to be sent home. However, her employer would not sign her exit visa. So the government would not let her go.

"Do you have anyone that you can stay with while your case is pending? Anyone to go to?" an official asked her.

She shook her head. There was no one.

"All right. You must stay at your embassy."

There, in that crowded, bleak box reeking with hopelessness, Yanu eked out her days. Months passed. The embassy of Nepal is not an elegant or spacious place. The walls hemmed Yanu in. She paced.

Because she was there so long, the embassy allowed her to live in a sort of extension run by Christians. Here there is a daily worship service. Girls are not required to come to the service, but nearly all do. The embassy tends to send Christian maids if there are any, so many of the detainees in that extension are Christians already. They worship, they sing, and they talk and learn about God and Jesus and how we should live our lives. The volunteers try to get Bibles in the women's own languages.

At the extension, the women also learn English and other useful skills, and, if they want, they can have Bible studies together on their own. During this time Yanu also was able to do some maid service, working for families connected with the extension. This went on for nine months. During all those months, she could not leave the building.

Yet in this small place, Yanu's faith blossomed. In her home country she had wanted to learn more about the Christian faith, but she had never seen it lived out as much as she did here. She began to read the Bible every day on her own. On Saturdays she started taking the initiative to read the Bible to other women in the extension and talk with them about what it meant.

"I think I could be a minister like you," she shyly told one of the Christian volunteers.

After Yanu had spent nine months in the shelter, her mentors thought surely the government would allow her to depart now. They encouraged Yanu to leave the sanctuary of the embassy and return to the police. The case did not turn out as they had expected, however. Now Yanu is in prison. No one who knows her understands why. Apparently her employer wants to save face, or to get his pound of flesh. Consequently, she is serving a three-year sentence.

Yanu lives in a cell with eight women. Seven are foreigners like Yanu, and one is a local. The wardens are fair, but some of her fellow prisoners are scary.

"She's been a really good influence in the prison," says an embassy staffer who visits her. Yanu leads a small Bible study every day. A Christian volunteer visits her once every two weeks. It makes no sense to Yanu that she is there, yet even though so many things seem to have conspired against her, her whole attitude is contentment. "This is God's will," she says.

WHAT ABOUT ARTUR?

What about Artur? With all the wealth and harsh custom arrayed against him, where could he turn? Although the odds for success were not high, the Philippine envoy went to the emir, the ruler of the country. The ambassador pressed the case. After fifty-eight days, the metal gates were unlocked and Artur walked out into Lily's arms.

Artur and Lily were better prepared for this experience than many others might have been. In a sense, they had been living like soldiers for a long time. They knew how to combine zeal with discipline. It was a habit. They were familiar with the restrictions of long separations, as well as the weight of ministry on top of regular jobs.

Artur had moved to the Gulf ten years before Lily had. Why did they separate? They had small children, she had a job in the Philippines, and they could save more money this way. But it meant they only saw each other once a year when he wangled a trip home for a couple of weeks.

Anticipating the problems, the couple had faced them head-on. Before Artur went abroad they prayed fiercely and made serious commitments regarding priorities and temptations. Once separated, they set aside a fixed time every week when they prayed for each other simultaneously. Also, they both kept very busy in local churches, he in the Gulf and she in the Philippines.

Eventually Lily moved to the Gulf "so that the children would know their dad." Now that the children are grown and back in the Philippines, the family meets over Skype. Across the miles they celebrate communion together. Before anyone begins to Skype, they have bread and juice ready. The parents gather the food at their end. The children gather the food at theirs. Then the family shares the Lord's Supper even though they are separated by many time zones and diverse cultures.

So Artur and Lily know something about living in challenging circumstances. Ministry presents still more challenges, especially for "tentmakers," those who have full-time jobs in the secular world. But they welcomed these challenges. "Before he was taken, we had prayed over the flat. We anointed it. We asked the Lord to cover it. We prayed over each other as husband and wife. So when it happened, I was able to continue going through my daily routine in my body as if it was normal, even though it was exactly abnormal," Lily says.

They also knew that throughout history Christians have spent time in jail. How many of the New Testament books were written in prison! If the Apostle Paul had not been incarcerated, or if the Apostle John had not been exiled, when would they have found time to write? When we read Romans or Revelation, we would do well to think about that. Centuries later, one of the most famous Christian classics of all time, *Pilgrim's Progress,* was written in a prison cell by John Bunyan. From Martin Luther King to Nelson Mandela to contemporary Christian Vietnamese, Chinese, Pakistanis, Iranians, and Malays, people continue to experience detention because of their faith and conscience.

When Artur was released, the couple breathed a great sigh of relief, and turned again to each other, to their jobs, and to their ministry. They thought the case was closed. However, several months later, formal charges were filed. One charge concerns money. A network of fellowship groups has been raising money for a building. They have identified the land and the project design. Slowly they are proceeding through the legal requirements. According to Lily, the church has documents to show that the money trail is legal and the funds collected can be accounted for. The charge of financial fraud can be proven to be unfounded. However, there are three other charges, and those concern "defamation of religion."

Lily is not fazed. "I am rejoicing in the Lord. I have learned how to live through persecution. My life is complete. Because of all my experience so far, I know now that I can take strength from the Bible. I can even say I'm proud of what happened, because if not for the Lord I would have been helpless."

So she preaches. She pays the taxi fare for an abused woman when no one else can. She stands with those who need an advocate. She counsels cross-culturally. She offers a listening ear—and soap and shampoo—to those who are detained. She steps into the pulpit yet again to give the people the word of the Lord. And the people say, "You shine so bright when you preach. And somebody seems to be standing by your side."

Bible Study Discussion Guide

1. Did suffering and persecution stop Lily's ministry?

2. How did Lily and Artur prepare in advance for their tough time? What strategies helped Lily during the jail period?

3. What did Lily learn through this suffering? In what way did she come to understand the Apostle Paul better?

4. Think about Yanu. How did her time in prison help her grow in her faith? How did she respond to her unjust imprisonment?

Read and discuss this text about
SUFFERING:
Hebrews 11:8–39

"W hat an ugly girl! So dark." Those were Auntie Elvira's comments whenever she looked at Maya.

"Not very smart, either," her other auntie, Dora, would pronounce.

Although Maya's father had died when she was six, her uncle volunteered to send her to college.

"Why bother? She won't finish. She won't be able to pass," her aunties warned.

Maya felt sliced to pieces inside when she heard her aunts' criticisms. But she studied faithfully, and graduated with a degree in nursing. Later she passed her national nursing board examination.

"Are you sure she really passed?" one aunt asked the other skeptically. "I didn't think she had the ability."

But Maya breathed, *Thank you, God,* even though she didn't know God personally. Then, because she wanted to help her mother economically, she took a job in the Arabian Gulf.

With a low self-concept and few social skills, Maya did not make close friends in that faraway place. Sometimes even her roommates treated her badly. In those days, the nurses did not have access to internet or Skype. Maya could only write to her mother by hand. When her tears fell, she had to be careful that they did not blot the page. She felt so alone.

BLINDED AND RAPED

Being demeaned is something that countless women throughout history have experienced. They have been underpaid, passed over, marginalized, exploited, and abused. Consider Angela, for example. While Maya was crippled by shaming, Angela was attacked physically.

When Angela showed up one day at the embassy door, it was clear that she had suffered a beating. A physical exam revealed both old and fresh bruises and burn marks across her body. Both of her hands were swollen and some of her fingers were broken, as was her nose.

Throughout her employment, Angela's employers had slammed her head against the wall, partly strangled her, pounded her feet until they bled, burned her with a flat iron, kicked her, deprived her of food and of contact with her own family members, refused to pay her salary, and threatened death.

What caused Angela to run away was that her employer had tried to gouge out her eyes. She escaped through a door that happened to be unlocked, a rare occurrence. An Asian couple helped her get to her embassy. Both her eyes were bleeding, and all she could see was darkness. To this day, she remains partially blind.

Angela thinks this happened because two of her employer's sons are blind. Perhaps the woman's pain and frustration provoked her to try to blind Angela. This story was reported in the *Kuwait Times.*

Rape may also be a danger, as we have seen in several women's stories. It can come from men in the household, colleagues at work, or men on the street. Elena was a nurse and a new believer in Jesus. She lived about a block from the hospital where she was employed. Walking to work one day, she was grabbed and stuffed into a pickup with four men. She was taken into the desert and raped. After three hours she was set free.

She came back to the hospital in a state of shock. Another rape victim took her into her care, and counselled and discipled her. Today Elena can smile again.

"Are you doing OK? Is there still a struggle for forgiveness?" Charis asks Elena whenever they get together.

"A little, but I'm coming along."

Although Elena has forgiven her rapists, she wants justice. The government investigation has concluded that there was no physical evidence of rape.

"Elena, that's a big lie!" Charis exclaims. "But even if the government won't admit it, God knows the truth."

Later Charis comments, "Sometimes this is a horrible place. That's why we need to be here. If not for people who can offer encouragement, this would be hell." Then she adds, "But when people come to Christ, they do learn to forgive."

A subtler kind of sexual harassment may happen in offices. Filipinas smile and raise their eyebrows and giggle. Local Arab men think this is flirting. Filipinas don't wear loose black robes over their clothes. As a people, Filipinos like to party. Some Filipinas do enter into sexual affairs.

At a more general level, migrant workers are viewed as tools to be used. And because some overseas workers take jobs as laborers or maids, there is a tendency to view *all* migrants as peons.

"The last company I worked in was difficult," one secretary explains. "The manager made suggestive comments, even on the phone. 'How beautiful you are. Will you go out with me? Every time I see you, you make me hot.'" He would touch his private parts when she would go to report to him. Sometimes she had to call her husband: "Come early. I need you to get me right now."

Another secretary repeatedly had to protest her boss's suggestions and wandering hands. "Sir, this is against my faith, even though I am single. And as for you, I know you are a family man. It would be better for you to terminate my employment than to go on like this. It's *haram*, forbidden by God."

"OK, no harm done," he would say. But the next day it would be the same story.

In another office, a manager ordered his secretary, "You're a Christian, not a Muslim, so take off your jacket." Often managers want secretaries to go out with them socially and get loose.

"Not all Filipinas are the same," Bolet told her manager. She shared the word of God with him to explain why she would not party wildly or dress suggestively.

Exploitation of women is by no means universal in the Gulf. Among the Arab citizens there are happy women, such as the elegantly gliding students and professors wearing silky black headdresses on some university campuses. Ordinary housewives and teenagers take joy in their work and their friends. Women do not cringe away from men, although they normally go out in groups and at times and in places that are considered appropriate.

Nor is the Gulf the only place where rape is a reality. It slithers through the US military, and indeed has been an issue between men and women throughout time. However, it is a sad truth that rape is a particular threat in this part of the world.

THE WORTH OF A WOMAN

Today almost 50 percent of the world's migrant workers are women. In her book *Global Women*, Barbara Ehrenreich writes about the growing "feminization of labor" (2004). Women feel pressure to work overseas to provide money for their families back home, even though frequently they are paid less than men.

Care is one of women's special contributions, Ehrenreich asserts. Whether in homes or hospitals, or even hotels and offices, women often add a personal dimension that enriches the people around them. Care should be viewed as a valuable commodity in the world today because there is a "care deficit" in rich countries, Ehrenreich says. Care should be treasured as the "new gold." Wealthy countries extract physical resources from poor countries, like oil and minerals. They also extract human resources, particularly caring women. Such women ought to be valued and paid accordingly, Ehrenreich contends. We should value care as one of our most precious resources, and note where it comes from and where it ends up.

Before the development of oil, wealth in the Arabian Gulf often came from pearls. Generations of villagers spent several months each year diving to dangerous depths. This was Kuwait's major industry until the 1930s, when the Japanese developed cultured pearls. As a result of that Japanese innovation, Gulf incomes crashed. What a lifesaver it was when oil was discovered here within a decade of the collapse of pearling.

Swirls of iridescence and hints of pink and blue shimmering in faint lines and layers in one little ball: that is the allure of a pearl. A smooth loveliness shines until it almost glows. Restrained elegance and understated beauty combine with brilliant hints of fire below the surface. A pearl is a mystery. In that sense, a pearl is very much like a woman. Every woman has layers of intricate design and a unique kind of beauty. Every woman is a treasure.

Jesus affirmed that. When he was on earth, he encountered a variety of women. Some had dubious futures. One day, for example, Jesus was accosted by an anxious man named Jairus.

"My daughter is dying. She's just twelve years old. Would you be willing to come see her at my house?" Jairus begged.

Jesus accompanied Jairus home. When they arrived, however, they walked into the grief and mourning of the girl's funeral.

Jesus was abrupt. "Clear out! This girl isn't dead. She's sleeping."

Sarcasm rained down on him. What an absurd statement.

Jesus ignored it. "Girl, get up," he said.

And she did.

To add complexity, there is another woman who shows up in this story recorded in Luke 8. While Jesus was walking toward Jairus' home, he encountered this second woman. She, too, was sick. For twelve years blood had been seeping out of her. No doctors had been able to help, but they had taken all her money. By now she was economically broke, physically anemic, psychologically burned out, and spiritually polluted, according to local beliefs. No doubt she stank.

In contrast to Jairus, who had run into Jesus' presence articulate and assertive, this downtrodden woman did not have the confidence to speak a word. What was the use? She just reached out and touched the hem of Jesus' robe.

Jesus sensed it. He turned and spoke to her. He took the initiative. She did not have to beg. Then after more than a decade of shame, confusion, stigma, and despair, she was healed.

What is a woman? Some societies see women primarily as property. Or cheap labor. Or sex objects for men's gratification. Or lineage connectors through their fathers or through their offspring. Or social stabilizers. Or they may view women negatively as dangerous pollutants. Christians see a woman as
- a human being created in the image of God
- potentially liberated by Jesus' death and resurrection
- potentially empowered by the Holy Spirit
- commissioned for active service in God's world

When Jesus met Jairus' daughter, he saw something special. Those around her had limited expectations. But Jesus saw that this girl had potential. She just needed to be awakened and empowered to get up. In the same way, he healed and liberated the unnamed middle-aged woman because he saw that the second half of her life mattered too. She still had a future. Forty times in the gospels Jesus interacted with women or made them the main characters in his stories, and he always treated them with respect.

LOVE IS POWER

Throughout history women empowered by God's love have blessed people. In the nineteenth century, for example, there was a remarkable outpouring of women's energies in mission. When this was celebrated in 1910, it was discovered that North American women had founded, were administering, and were supporting over forty women's overseas Christian mission agencies, undergirding over 2,500 women missionaries, 6,000 indigenous Bible women, 3,263 schools, 80 hospitals, 11 colleges, and innumerable orphanages and dispensaries, according to historian Dana Robert (1996). Similar women's missions movements pulsated on other continents.

What motivated these women? Experiencing God's love was key, right across the denominations. Early Pentecostal theologian Minnie Abrams published *The Baptism of the Holy Ghost & Fire* in 1906. Here she developed a "missiology of divine love." When a person receives the baptism of the Holy Spirit, Abrams taught,

> The fire of God's love will so burn within you that you will
> desire the salvation of souls. You will accept the Lord's
> commission to give witness and realize that he to whom
> all power is given has imparted some of that power to you,
> sufficient to do all that he has called you to do. (44)

"The prominent healing and compassion ministries of Pentecostals in the twentieth century were largely the product of women, an indirect offshoot of the missiology of divine love first espoused by Minnie Abrams," according to Robert (1996).

In the same way, "holiness" churchwomen—Methodists, Wesleyans, Nazarenes—were propelled outward when they experienced God's love. They felt liberated, strengthened, and even compelled to step into the public arena. In the holiness tradition,

> mission work . . . required the special consecration and
> sacrificial submission to God's will that could be obtained
> through an experience of "perfect love" [a holiness
> distinctive]. Such an experience was also important to
> give women the confidence they needed to travel around

speaking and organizing on behalf of missions. . . . [It]
provided the means of their own liberation from fear of
public speaking, financial management, and traveling alone.
. . . They felt freed from the silence imposed on them by
American society and they began to speak out in church and
to commit themselves to social service and mission work on
behalf of others. (Robert 1996, 140, 144–48)

In "mainline" denominations, as well, God's love moved
women. Mary Lyon founded Mt. Holyoke College as a "female
seminary" in 1837. Fifty years later, Mt. Holyoke alumnae
constituted 20 percent of the missionary women connected with
the American Board of Commissioners for Foreign Missions.
President Lyon trained women to use their time and manage
their small financial resources well so that they would have
something to give for mission. Biology was not destiny in her
school. But Lyon taught more than a system. She insisted that
it was God's love and God's presence with us that gives us the
courage to act. In a graduation address, she said,

You will find no pleasure like the pleasure of active effort. . . .
Never be hasty to decide that you can not do, because you
have not physical or mental strength. Never say you have no
faith or hope. Always think of God's strength when you feel
your weakness, and remember that you can come nearer to
him than to any being in the universe. We have desired to
educate you to go among the rich or the poor, to live in the
country or the village, in New England, the West, or in a
foreign land. And, wherever you are, remember that God
will be with you. (Fiske 1886, 85–86)

Across the denominations, nineteenth-century women were
conscious of weakness, timidity, lack of resources, and lack of

confidence. In this very weakness, however, they experienced the dynamizing love of God.

And shy, downtrodden, self-deprecating Maya became a woman like that too.

MAYA'S STORY

Reeling from her aunts' criticism, but determined to earn more money in order to help her mother, Maya had gone to the Middle East. In spite of the fact that it was illegal to bring a Bible into the country where she worked, Maya had packed one in her suitcase. She felt a hunger for God. As a child she had wondered, "Why are there so many saints in church? There's only one God." Even in those early years she sensed somehow that God was calling her.

Now, when her first dorm room didn't work out well, Maya transferred to another. Here she discovered that several of her new roommates were "born again." They had Christian fellowship meetings in the room.

"I have a Bible, but I don't really know it. What's in the Bible?" Maya wondered.

During the months that followed, she learned what was in that book. Above all, she heard the gospel of grace. One year went by. She attended Bible study regularly. Her homesickness dissolved. She gained friends and came to know Jesus Christ through them. Around her neck she had always worn a sacred medal on a chain. It was supposed to keep her safe. One day she lifted the chain over her head, and set it aside on her dresser. This was Maya's way of showing that she trusted in Jesus. She didn't need the talisman's protection anymore.

Gradually Maya gained the courage to talk in front of people. "It was easier because they were all girls, and even girls were teaching," she said. She also learned to pray. At first it seemed strange. She didn't know how. But eventually she was praying for long periods, sometimes two hours at a time.

Maya was baptized in a bathtub, with women officiating.

When she went home for a visit, her mother was upset about these developments. Maya tried to explain, but wasn't very successful. So when she returned to the Gulf, she tried to obey her mother and keep away from the Bible study. But she couldn't sleep.

It's heavy for me. Lord, just help me. I want to follow you, not the born-again way, not the Catholic way, but I want to hear from you, she prayed.

She remembered the parable about how the seed-word planted in fertile soil would be multiplied. When she read this again, she cried. "I want to multiply!"

Maya telephoned her mother. "I don't have peace without the Bible study, Mom."

"Where you have peace, that's where you should go," her mother decided.

So for five years Maya grew with the Bible study there. "Then the Lord transferred me elsewhere where I would grow up and have more salary."

TWO ARE BETTER THAN ONE

Lord, two heads are better than one, Maya breathed. Years had passed. They had been fruitful. Now, at age 35, Maya was ready for the love and companionship of a man, the joy of children, and the strength that she and a partner could give to each other in ministry. *Lord, could you bring me a husband,* she prayed, *and could he be a pastor?* In the Middle East migrant context, being a pastor usually meant holding a secular job as well as having the calling and passion and motivation to pastor people.

Meanwhile, back home in the Philippines there was a pastor named Ben who was praying that God would send him a wife who was a missionary.

Maya went home on leave to the Philippines and traveled around to churches as a sort of missionary, encouraging them. Although she was shy, she could talk boldly about the word of God. Every time she stepped out, she said, *Lord, I will not go without you.* And every time, God supplied what she needed.

"What is your priority in a husband?" a mentor asked her after she confessed her desire to be married.

"I want spiritual strength," Maya decided.

She told her pastor about her desire for a pastor-husband. Her pastor in turn introduced Maya to Ben, and assigned Ben to escort her to various churches. As they got to know each other, Maya came to admire him. But he was so quiet. He did not talk much at all. This bothered her. *Lord, if he will not talk, we will have too much silence,* she murmured.

Eventually her scheduled meetings were coming to a close. She needed to move on. *Lord, this is my last day to go to churches here. What shall I do?* she prayed. *I guess I'll go back to the Middle East if this man does not talk.*

Ben was thinking along the same lines. He was remembering that again and again God had provided what he had asked for. On the very day when Maya was coming to the end of her rope, and deciding to go back to the Gulf, Ben heard God speak. "Remember when you needed money? I provided it. Then when you needed a vehicle? I provided." Case by case, the Lord reminded him of his provision. Then the silent voice said, "Now you have been praying for a partner, a wife. And I am giving you one. But *you are not talking to her!*"

So Ben said to Maya, "Let's eat."

Over lunch he told her what the Lord had said.

"Why are you telling me? Who are you talking about as this 'partner'? Me?" she asked.

"Yes."

She lifted her eyes to him. "I've been praying for a pastor husband."

When they walked out of the restaurant, they were holding hands.

"Why?" she asked, looking at their linked hands. "Are we boyfriend and girlfriend already?"

"Yes. We'll be engaged for one year," he said. And that is what happened.

As the wedding day approached, Maya asked the Lord for a special sign. *Lord, let him give me white roses!*

The youth were scheduled to sing "Power of Love" at the ceremony. As they practiced the day before the wedding, Maya watched. During this rehearsal, the singers surprised her by coming up to her one by one. Each gave her a white rose. To Maya this was God's over-the-top assurance that he would be with them in their marriage. They would be secure. God would be there.

Ben didn't have a job when they returned to the Gulf as a newly married couple. Six months later, however, he was a manager on an American base as well as a volunteer pastor for Filipinos and others. Being a pastor's wife has been an adjustment for Maya, even though that was what she had wanted. Now that several years have passed, they have two children. One of them was born with Down's syndrome.

"After confirming this condition, I didn't ask God why," Maya says. *Just show me how to take care of him,* I asked. God has a purpose for everything."

Today if you see Maya and Ben together, there is a bounce in their step and a twinkle in their eyes when they look at each other. "He complements my weaknesses," she says.

A WARRIOR FOR WOMEN

"Who is your favorite Bible character?" I asked Maya.

"Deborah," she answered.

I was surprised. Who was Deborah?

In the years between God's people's captivity in Egypt and the establishment of the kingdom, alien armies sometimes threatened them. Deborah was living when one of those crises arose. "What can we do? Who will help?" people cried. When no man rose up to lead the people in a defensive action, Deborah said, "I'll do it. I'll lead." She did. The campaign was successful, and the people were saved.

But Maya—as Deborah?

"Deborah is my favorite Bible character. I see her as a strong women," Maya said. "When I was single, I became strong through the grace of God. For example, I experienced that strength when I had an accident here. I banged a Muslim woman's car. She talked against me harshly. I had no family here—I was not yet married."

A complaint was lodged against Maya in court, delaying her regular trip home.

"When I went to the hearing, I just prayed to God. One friend stayed home and interceded for me. I saw the judge as if he was the Lord Jesus. All of them were talking in Arabic and I didn't understand. There was one big window of glass. It reminded me of heaven. *Where will my help come from?* I thought. *From the maker of heaven and earth.* I held on to that."

"Was it your fault?" the judge asked her.

"Yes," she answered.

"Just don't have an accident for three months," he ruled. And Maya was free to travel home right away.

Earlier various people had urged her to pay a bribe or contact a captain for special influence. A policeman had offered to sign for her in the hearing, which would have been legal. But Maya had forgotten to contact him, and God worked it out anyway.

"Deborah became strong because of the Lord. And before God called me I was weak and could not do anything, could not stand in front of others, my knees would tremble and my voice would tremble."

Now, instead of cowering, Maya makes visits to nurses' dorms and goes from room to room, introducing herself. "How are you? Do you have some free time?" Eventually she tells them about her experience with Jesus.

"I introduce Jesus' love," she says. "I have a burden for these girls. I try to teach them God's plan for them."

There is a lot of immorality going on, she says. Women turn to men for comfort, but it is fleeting. Some of the men are married already, yet they lie in order to get girlfriends.

While she was single, and now that she is married, Maya has started Bible studies in the dorms. Men neither distract nor police the women there, because they are prohibited from entering. This provides a training ground for women who want to grow.

"I don't have talent. I'm not that smart," Maya says. "But I want to encourage other girls that even if you're not outstanding, if you will give everything to the Lord, he will teach you and use you."

Some women are hardened. Others are afraid of religion. "I used to be like that," Maya tells them. "I used to pretend that I was asleep when people talked about Jesus. But, in any case, religion cannot save you. When you face the Lord after death, he will not ask you what your religion is."

One girl in the Bible study had had two children with two different fathers, and both men were married to women back home. Through the study, this woman decided not to sleep around with men anymore. Another woman, a lesbian, separated from her partner as a result of the Bible study.

Muslims have asked Maya what is in the Bible, and she has explained it to them. A Hindu woman accepted a card from Maya that described God's plan for people. The Hindu girl went into the bathroom to read it privately. As she read, God's spirit worked on her and she began to shiver. After that, she started attending church, and in time became a Christian, faithfully praising God throughout the whole time she worked in the Gulf.

One girl had a good singing voice. Maya took her to church. The worship music team leader wanted this girl to join the platform group, and urged Maya to be part of the team too.

"But my voice goes left and right," Maya confessed.

"What's important is not your voice but what is in your heart," the leader responded.

So Maya became a backup singer. Sometimes, however, she ended up having to sing the echo refrain by herself. How she wished for a partner to sing along with her, because she knew her own voice was not reliable.

Yet one day someone said to her, "Sister Maya, did you hear those other voices? It was as though angels were singing with you!"

Apparently God had sent some partner voices after all.

In a milieu where women's life is hard and sometimes even dangerous, this shy woman of little value to others has blossomed into a Deborah, a caring women, a beautiful pearl in God's kingdom. Her favorite verse is Romans 8:28: "In all things God works for the good of those who love him, who have been called according to his purpose."

Bible Study Discussion Guide

1. How does this shy woman's development encourage you? What are your own limitations?

2. Think of women you know who have low self-concepts. How might this story encourage them?

3. How did Jesus view women? Give several examples.

4. How has the Christian faith empowered women? Give a historic example.

5. "Care is the new gold." What does this mean? How should we view women who work in "caring" jobs?

6. Thank God for the ways he loves women and the ways he loves you in particular.

Read and discuss these texts about
GOD'S CARE FOR A DESPISED WOMAN:
Genesis 16:1–2,7–13 and 21:9–20

Humans are on a journey beyond our earthly plane. According to the Bible, we are traveling from the garden of Eden to an eternal destination. There is a route we must follow. The way is long, narrow, and often perilous. Those who make it ultimately will arrive at heaven, the city of God.

The women featured in this book are pilgrims to that city.

Most of the stories told here begin with brokenness and a sense of loss—separation from family, disconnection from culture, and lack of material wealth. We also read about these workers' lofty ambitions and goals amid their struggles. Some stories begin as failures. Yet all describe a journey toward an eschatological destination. Along the way, the women whose stories are gathered here find their status as daughters of the King of kings, co-heirs with Christ, and citizens of heaven.

THE AWESOME CIRCUIT

The feminization of overseas foreign workers is not new. Filipinas offer an example. As vividly described in chapter 2, they answer the call of wealth resounding from the oil-drenched Arabian Gulf. Outsiders might be tempted to view this as a cluster of personal responses, individuals migrating in order to better their own economic situations. However, the Overseas Foreign Worker (OFW) program is an official Philippine government institution that is more than three decades old.

Filipino workers now have migrated to over two hundred countries. This outpouring, and specifically the flood to the Arabian Gulf states, began shortly after the vastness of the Arabian oil reserves was announced to the world. In 1974, President Ferdinand Marcos signed Presidential Decree 442 "to ensure the careful selection of Filipino workers for overseas labor markets (and) to protect the good name of the Philippines abroad." During the 1970s and 1980s, the "petrodollar" phenomenon dominated world attention. The oil-producing nations controlled the supply of energy. It was during this period that the Philippines' outsourcing of labor began. Eventually 10 percent of employed Filipino citizens would be working overseas and sending earnings back home. The labor migration policy of the Marcos administration became an essential element in nation-building, and has been embraced by succeeding administrations up to the present.

According to the official 2012 documents of the Commission on Filipinos Overseas, over two million Filipinos are working in the oil-rich Arabian Peninsula:

Kingdom of Saudi Arabia—1,267,658
United Arab Emirates—931,562
Bahrain—66,491
Oman—51,065
Qatar—200,016
Kuwait—213,638

Many of these workers from the Philippines are women: mothers, grandmothers, aunts, daughters. They include both married and single women. They are accountants, teachers, nurses, dentists, storekeepers, managers, secretaries, and maids. Left behind are friends, families, communities, and "roots." The migrants are transplanted to unknown foreign lands where they must learn to embrace new cultures. Some will return to their homeland as planned. For many others, contracts will be extended or new work sponsors will delay their homecoming.

It is an awesome journey, but a million Filipinas have embarked on it. So have women from many other nations.

THE CITY OF GOD

In the last book of the Bible, the Christian's final destination, heaven, is described as "[shining] with the glory of God . . . its brilliance . . . like that of a very precious jewel, like jasper, clear as crystal." Revelation 21–22 reveals many more sparkling details. This place is governed by absolute righteousness, justice, and peace. Who would not want to live forever in such a city?

Though the migrants working in the Gulf region often are despised as lowly laborers, the women in this book are on a journey to heaven, the city of God, the "New Jerusalem." Even if they start their journey owning almost nothing, and even if they must struggle through sufferings, still they hold on to this assurance:

> Those who hope in the Lord
> will renew their strength.
> They will soar on wings like eagles.
> They will run and not grow weary,
> They will walk and not be faint.
> (Isa 40:31)

Yet these women pilgrims are not just concerned with their own personal progress. They also point others to the "narrow road" that leads to the city of God. They provide instruction and inspiration to other pilgrims. They serve as guides and lampposts. They warn travelers of danger zones and hazardous temptations that may lead to destruction. With other migrants and even with their hosts, they share the good news about the city that is to come.

In God's sovereignty, these pilgrims find resting places within the community of Christians wherever they may be. Such local churches and fellowships are invaluable. There may also be other benefactors. In each Gulf state that we visited, we encountered a figure we call Baba, meaning "papa." This person provided a shelter for the foreign followers of Jesus where they could worship and fellowship. Often this was in his home or compound. All the Babas we met have been of the Muslim faith. Although not Christian, their lives have been touched by the Christian community in some way. Some have been exposed to Christian employees and household staff for a long time. Some have been blessed by the love and generosity of Christian teachers or nurses.

During the period of Exile in Hebrew history, there were Persians who took care of God's chosen people. Possibly something like that is happening here through the Babas. Sometimes God works in mysterious ways. Only in heaven will we understand it all. Meanwhile, as we consider these Babas and the households who have shown hospitality in inhospitable situations, we wonder if there are ways to minister to them. Surely the migrants whom they bless can be a blessing to them also.

WHERE DO WE GO FROM HERE?

The writers of this book look forward to the day when the nations will assemble in the city of God, as described in Revelation 21. Meanwhile, through these stories we have become aware of sisters who live and work in difficult places in our time. How might we respond to this reality? How might we reach out to them in Christian love and solidarity?

Here are a few recommendations to start us on our journey together.

- Work on ministries of hospitality. If the church is the pilgrim's earthly home, how can the Christian community extend welcome? Recognize the significance of hospitality in fulfilling God's mission.
- Connect abused and persecuted workers with advocacy and justice organizations in order to safeguard their rights and well-being.
- Provide pastoral care for the families of diaspora people left behind in the homelands.
- Provide intercultural orientation for workers before they go.
- As well as teaching them how to learn a new culture, work skills, and coping skills, train every Christian in basic spiritual disciplines, in Islam, in gracious and effective witness, in discipling a new Christian, and in confronting temptations and discouragement.
- For those who may pastor Christian fellowships abroad even as they work in secular jobs, give them theological and ministry training before they go. Focus on some of the issues discussed in this book: discipleship, advocacy, marriage and family counseling, and ministry to members of "unreached peoples" who are present among the migrants in the Gulf.
- Nurture strategic partnership of like-minded organizations and institutions to increase access in the Gulf to evangelistic resources (the JESUS film,

Scripture portions, etc.), especially in languages of difficult-to-reach peoples (like Pakistanis) whose members also are working in the region. Such partnerships can also help supply practical resources like toiletries and recreational income-generating materials for those who minister to women taking sanctuary in embassies.

- Pray on your own, and develop prayer networks to pray on a regular basis for women foreign workers, their families, their employers, and their communities.

God moves. He moves the galaxies and the seasons. He moves the tides of the oceans and all the creatures in their depths. He moves the development of an infant into a runabout toddler and into a strapping, brilliant young man. God is in action, in motion. For one lifetime God moved from heaven to live in a human body on earth. There is something lovely about settling down, and Micah 4:4 beautifully portrays the heavenly time when every man will relax contentedly beside his own vine and fig tree, without needing to get up and travel onward. But at present many people must leave home, journeying from one country to another. As they do, they should know that God moves too.

And wherever we go, God is there already. He owns the Arabian Gulf, and every other place in the world where we might head. God is the Creator of all, the Sustainer of all, the Originator of moral law and wisdom for all, the Model of compassion and mercy and love for all. God is the one who will culminate the history of every land and every people.

In our time in the twenty-first century, God is choosing to use some of the least powerful people in the great sweep of human labor exchanges—migrant working women—and through them God is giving glimpses of his grace.

Bible Study Discussion Guide

1. Review how migrant workers are growing as Jesus' disciples. Give examples from some of the stories in this book.

2. Review how migrant workers are reaching out in witness and service.

3. Think about the challenges of youth ministry, church planting, and theological education among migrant workers. How could your favorite mission help provide resources for migrant workers in these areas?

4. Today migrant workers are on every continent. Could you reach out to those who work in your city or country?

5. What are we destined for? Where are human beings headed? Does this encourage you? How?

Read and discuss these texts about
OUR FUTURE:
Revelation 21:1–6,22–27 and 22:1–6

Abrams, Minnie. 1906. *The Baptism of the Holy Ghost & Fire.* 2nd ed. Kedgaon: Mukti Mission Press.

Adeney, Miriam. 2009. *Kingdom without Borders: The Untold Story of Global Christianity.* Downer's Grove, IL: InterVarsity.

Ehrenreich, Barbara, and Arlie Russell Hochschild. 2003. *Global Woman: Nannies, Maids, and Sex Workers in the New Economy.* New York: Metropolitan.

Fiske, Fidelia. 1886. *Recollections of Mary Lyon, with Selections from Her Instructions to the Pupils in Mt. Holyoke Female Seminary.* Boston: American Tract Society.

Lausanne Committee for World Evangelization. 2010. *Scattered to Gather: Embracing the Global Trend of Diaspora.* Manila: LifeChange Publishing.

Pantoja, Luis, Jr., Sadiri Joy Tira, and Enoch Wan. 2004. *Scattered: The Filipino Global Presence.* Manila: LifeChange Publishing.

Robert, Dana L. 1996. *American Women in Mission: A Social History of Their Thought and Practice.* Macon, GA: Mercer University Press.

Rynkiewich, Michael A. 2011. *Soul, Self, and Society: A Postmodern Anthropology for Mission in a Postcolonial World.* Eugene, OR: Cascade Books.

Sunquist, Scott W. 2013. *Understanding Christian Mission: Participation in Suffering and Glory.* Grand Rapids, MI: Baker Academic.

Thompson, Andrew. 2010. *The Christian Church in Kuwait: Religious Freedom in the Gulf.* Kuwait: Saeed and Sameer.

Yergin, Daniel. 2008. *The Prize: The Epic Quest for Oil, Money, and Power.* 3rd ed. New York: Free Press.